WITNESS TO CHANGE

AUTOBIOGRAPHY OF AN ACADEMIC ECONOMIST

MATTHEW DRENNAN

ISBN: 978-0-578-39970-6

Library of Congress Control Number: 2022905782

Contents

Introduction

Although I was raised as a Catholic in the 1940s and trained as a Ph.D. economist in the 1960s, I witnessed a lot of change over the past four decades. At the beginning of my life as an economist, I sneered at the other social sciences for not being rigorous, and I belittled other Christian faiths as too squishy. I wanted certainty. What I most liked about Catholicism was its clarity in holding the individual to blame for sins, not parents, not teachers, not society. What I liked most about neoclassical economics was its clarity that the rational consumer and the rational producer would irrevocably reach the best rational outcome with no need for government interference. And that could be demonstrated on a blackboard. I was a true believer. But I was also a natural skeptic, so the crash was inevitable. However my crash was slow moving, not sudden. That is the story I tell here.

Chapter One

Why This Book

In December 1961 I heard Paul Samuelson's presidential address at the annual meeting of the American Economic Association in New York. He was the most outstanding economist of that era. He later became the first American recipient of the Nobel Memorial Award in economics. I had moved to New York in the summer of 1961 after completing my Master of Arts studies in economics at the University of Michigan.

I loved his speech then. Today I do not. Samuelson was an elegant, gifted writer, a rare characteristic among economists. In his speech, he praised past economists who had advanced economic analysis, such as Walras, Cournot, and Quesnay, none of whom were known outside the profession. He discounted (some might say trashed) some famous economists noted for big ideas but not for economic analysis, such as Karl Marx, Henry George, Thorstein Veblen, and John Kenneth Galbraith. Samuelson ended his speech with this exhortation to his audience of economists:

> "Not for us is the limelight and the applause. But that doesn't mean the game is not worth the candle or that we do not in the end win the game. In the long run the economic scholar works for the only coin worth having—our own applause." (*American Economic Review*, March 1962, p. 18)

To me, today, his exhortation sounds the retreat of economics from real world economic problems. He modified his view in a footnote to the published version of his speech, but the audience, including me, didn't hear his footnote:

> "Lest I be misunderstood, I elaborate. This is not a plea for 'Art for its own sake, 'Logical elegance for the sake of elegance. It is not a plea for leaving the real-world problems of political economy to noneconomists. It is not a plea for short-run popularity with members of a narrow in-group. Rather it is a plea for calling shots as they really appear to be (on reflection and after weighing all evidences), even when this means losing popularity with the great audience of men and running against 'the spirit of the times.'" (*Ibid, ff 11*)

As a Ph.D. graduate student in economics at New York University beginning in 1965, I along with the other economics graduate students embraced Samuelson's message because it was the same one delivered by our professors, especially the younger ones. There was a pecking order in the academic profession, and Kenneth Arrow and

Paul Samuelson were at the top. They were noted for their mathematical analysis of economic issues. Galbraith and Veblen were at the bottom—they were noted for their avoidance of mathematical analysis. Indeed, when my first wife gave me a copy of Galbraith's latest book for my birthday while I was in graduate school, I was quietly embarrassed and never read it. All of us graduate students in economics aspired to have a profound influence upon modern economic analysis, *not* on political economy. That meant more mathematics and statistics. When NYU replaced a second foreign language requirement for economics, with a few math and statistics courses, I eagerly jumped for that option.

All the rage in academic economics back then was Arrow and DeBreu's work on general equilibrium theory and Paul Samuelson's magnum opus, *Foundations of Economic Analysis.* As a child, I had nightmares that lasted until I was about seven. But they restarted in graduate school at NYU. The most vivid one I remember occurred when I was taking the third-level calculus course. I dreamed that I was a cosecant function being pursued by a monster determined to eat me. My only escape was to transform myself into the definite integral of a cosecant function, but I could not remember the definite integral of a cosecant function!

In graduate school I took a number of econometrics courses, the statistics workhorse of empirical analytical economics. Later, as an economics professor, most of my professional articles in urban and regional economics over four decades employed econometrics. And most of them address real world problems not addressed in neoclassical economics because their rigid assumptions assume away such problems.

What are the fervently held beliefs of neoclassical economists? To be sure, they would not call them "beliefs" but rather strong assumptions supporting their rigorously derived principles. This list covers their key beliefs:

1. Perfect competition prevails in every market, i.e. many buyers, many sellers, homogeneous product; no monopolies or oligopolies or government interference.

2. All consumers are rational and seek to maximize their utility within their income constraint.

3. All producers are rational and seek to maximize their profits.

4. Perfect information; all consumers and producers have access to the information required to make rational choices.

We all learned this in economics 101, and we all know that none of them is true. Let me explain and elaborate, one at a time.

1. **Perfect competition**. The only markets today that come close to having many buyers, many sellers, and homogeneous products are agricultural markets such as wheat and

soybeans. As history has shown us (the Progressive Era that established antitrust legislation), there is no way to have neither monopolies nor oligopolies (an oligopoly is a large firm or a few large firms that successfully keep out competitors) without government interference, i.e. regulation. But enacted regulation can be mitigated by lobbying the federal government (corporate lobbying in Washington exploded in size starting in the 1970s). The patent laws, meant to encourage innovation, effectively stifle it. Conservatives who celebrate perfect competition never decry corporate lobbying and patent laws that restrict perfect competition.

2. **Rational consumers.** The consumption theory of neoclassical economics imagines a consumer we have never known, i.e. indifferent to the buying choices of others. A parent who is confronted by a crying child returning from school who lacks (a) new Nike sneakers, (b) a color widescreen TV, (c) a cell phone, (d) whatever, will not be moved to buy those things by the crying child just because other parents buy them for their kids. Really? And such a consumer will keep their spending within their available income. The economy crashed in the Great Recession because of consumer debt for housing and medical care. Next time it will be because of student debt. Their available income is not sufficient, thanks in large part to rising income inequality. Also, as the new field of behavioral economics has demonstrated with

data and experiments, consumers are very often *not* rational. The economist and sociologist Thorstein Veblen had a better theory of consumption back in 1899, recognizing the importance of "conspicuous consumption." The success of advertising depends on conspicuous consumption.

3. **Rational producers.** It is a reasonable assumption that producers are rational but producers—big corporations—believe that their large spending on elections, and even larger spending on lobbying, will maximize their profits by restricting competition. This may indeed be true, but it contradicts assumption number one, perfect competition.

4. **Perfect information.** The Nobel economist Joseph Stiglitz has shown that perfect information for consumers and producers is sorely lacking.

Does it matter that these core beliefs or assumptions are false? Milton Friedman argued in a path-breaking article that real world economic outcomes demonstrated *as if* they are true. "[Friedman] chose to express his point of view by denying the need to base economic theories on so-called 'realistic' assumptions, asserting that 'as-if' assumptions will meet all our purposes . . ." (Blaug, *Economic History and the History of Economics,* pp. 265–266).

Those who came after him strengthened Friedman's position by admitting not all consumers and producers are rational, but applying the law of large numbers, the representative consumer and producer *are* rational.

This memoir tries to explain how I evolved from a true believer in mainstream neoclassical economics to a skeptic as I passed through academia at different universities. The economics profession moved to the right over the period covered here, 1961 to the present, while I moved to the left (not to the far left; not to Marxism or economic socialism).

This memoir also tries to explain my slow evolution from being a devout Catholic to a fallen-away Catholic. Note that my innate skepticism was central to both of those life changes.

But I need to tell you how I came to be an academic economist and how I started life as a practicing Catholic, and that requires going further back in time. The move away from being a devout Catholic came earlier than the move away from neoclassical economics. The parts about my growing skepticism are in short vignettes, unburdened with both the dismal science and Catholic theology. By recounting my journey through personal anecdotes, I hope to amuse you and keep you interested.

Chapter Two

Formative Years

We moved into the La Salle Boulevard house on the west side of Detroit in the fall of 1940 when I was going on three years old. I sat on our baby grand piano in a room empty of furniture except for a huge console radio, short wave, and phono which we were all focused upon. Some adult male relative was fussing with it to make it work. It did. In an empty closet my father held me up to swing on the bar. It was my home until I married in 1960.

I was lucky to be born into a supportive and loving family. The youngest of seven children, I was doted on by my five older sisters and my mother, Margaret. I have been told by them that when I was born they were delighted that I was a boy because the previous four births were all girls. My sisters and my mother were never unkind or indifferent. The only physical punishment I recall was a spanking from my mother around the age of seven for playing with the younger brother of a kid with the dreaded polio next door. Their house was under quarantine at that time. There were no serious quarrels or fights among my siblings that I recall all the years I lived at home.

The only dark cloud in my family was my father's drinking. One night when I was probably five years old, asleep in my parent's room, I was awakened by shouting. My mother, in her bathrobe, was screaming at my father (who disliked his name Mathias so called himself Matt), and he was screaming back. She threw one of her slippers at him. I cringed with dread and confusion. This had never happened before. I pretended to be asleep as their shouting continued. I do not recall what they were saying, but they were clearly angry. I heard my mother use the word "drunk." It frightened me and has stayed with me all these years. At the time I probably did not know what "drunk" meant. But as years passed, I learned. My father was often drunk when I was growing up. His drinking colored my life and that of the other younger kids: Marita, Paddy, and Joanie. The older ones—Peggy, Eddie, and Katie—were not living at home after 1945 so they were much less affected.

The rest of us were affected by his drinking. In addition to my two married sisters, we had many relatives and friends in Detroit. When we were invited to social events at their homes, none of us, including my mother, was eager to have my father accompany us when he was drunk, so we never even asked him to join us. My mother would make an excuse for his absence, usually that he was sick. To my married sisters, she did not need to make an excuse. They knew. But to most of our world, it was a dark secret never discussed—but probably inferred by many.

My father never physically abused my mother or any of us children. But he would yell a lot when he was drunk, which scared me. One night my mother was out, and my father was home drunk. He came into the bedroom where the four of us youngest were getting ready for bed. He started yelling at us, and Paddy, Joanie, and I began to cry. He kept yelling. Then Marita, the oldest of us four, seized a scissors, brandished it and shouted, "Get out of here *now*!" He stopped yelling and left the room. I was so relieved, as were Paddy and Joanie. Marita was our hero, our protector.

Even sober, my father was more distant than my mother. He never played games or sports with me and Joanie but he did take us to Tiger (baseball) and Lions (football) and Red Wings (hockey) games. To me, those were never as exciting as the movies. I knew I was supposed to like sports so I pretended that I did. The hockey games seemed interminable, especially when they cleared the ice with those big Zamboni machines between periods with dreadful organ music blaring.

Drunk or sober, my father, a salesman of Great Lakes sand had a booming voice. The rest of us spoke softly. One Sunday in early spring, after the lakes were free of ice and open for shipping, he drove us over to Canada where he had to observe a lake freighter take on a load of sand. After the ship was loaded and he finished his business with the captain, he took us to dinner in Canada at what were called roadhouses along the Detroit River. They served marvelous fresh lake fish and, best of all, frog legs which were deep fried. After dinner we began the drive along the river back to Detroit. Suddenly my father stopped the car and said, "The freighter is going the wrong way!" He jumped out and ran to the water's edge. He began shouting and waving his arms. His message got through. The great ship slowly made a U-turn (the river is a mile wide) and headed in the right direction. I am sorry for all the boys who do not have such a story about their fathers. Did Moses have a son who saw him part the waters?

Joanie and I, the youngest of the seven siblings, were probably the most affected by our father's drinking because we had no memory of his congenial sobriety in earlier years. That is when he frequented a neighborhood saloon, Harry's Bar. Harry became one of my father's best friends. Always present in his drinking establishment, along with his cocker spaniel dog, Bing, Harry would shout at the dog, "Sing, Bing." Bing would rise up on his back legs and howl. The patrons were delighted.

When the U.S. was in World War II, 1941 to 1945, there was strict gasoline rationing. Because of my father's connection to a side trucking business, he was given ration cards that allowed him to buy more gasoline than the allotted maximum for households. One consequence of his drinking was a lawsuit against him around 1946. His partner at the trucking firm claimed that my father did not fulfill his duties because he was so often drunk. To avoid a possible costly judgement, everything my father owned was transferred to my mother. I was only nine years old at the time. I am not certain of the outcome, but I know that nothing drastic happened. At dinner one night around this time, my parents and the older kids were grousing about the partner's lawsuit. Not wanting to be left out, I said with indignation, "Next time there is a war, we won't take any gasoline ration cards from *him*." My brother Eddie burst out laughing.

When Joanie and I were in high school, our father drank alone at home. When he wasn't drunk, he was allegedly "sick." Drunk or sick, he would hole up in his bedroom. The short periods when he was not drinking had this pattern: Joanie or I would drive him to his office in downtown Detroit on non-school days, our mother on school days. Around noon he would call home and ask to be picked up because he was sick. On the way home, he would insist on stopping off at his doctor's office for a prescription of phenobarbital. Years later when my adult sister Paddy accused that doctor of being my father's enabler, the doctor replied, "If I didn't give him phenobarbital he would drink more." I do not know what else my father's doctor was prescribing, but we all referred to his bedroom chifforobe as "the drugstore."

The contrast between the 1940s and 1950s social picture of the American father and my vivid experience of my own father made me an iconoclast for life. I think the same was true for my sister Joanie, and less so for my sister Paddy. Recently Paddy told me she felt pity for him. I felt contempt. As an obedient son, I never expressed my contempt to anyone but Joanie. This contempt for my father spilled over into in my popular music preferences. It was the era of maudlin Irish songs like "Oh Danny Boy," "Christmas in Killarney," and others sung by Bing Crosby and other crooners, and they made me gag. I liked the songs that featured Irish drunkenness and rowdy behavior, not because I celebrated them but because they conveyed the reality I experienced. For example, I knew all the words to "The Night that Paddy Murphy Died," but not to "Oh Danny Boy." Here is the beginning of the song I knew:

"Oh the night that Paddy Murphy died I never will forget
The Irish got so stinking drunk that some aren't sober yet.
The only thing they did that night that filled my heart with cheer
They took the ice right off the corpse
And put it in the beer!"
[chorus]
"Oh Lordy that's how they showed their respect for Paddy Murphy
That's how they showed their honor and their pride
That's how they showed their respect for Paddy Murphy,
Respect for Paddy Murphy on the night that Paddy died."

Not only was I an iconoclast but I was, early on, a contrarian. My father was one hundred percent Irish-American, my mother was fifty percent Irish and fifty percent German-American. They both despised the British, and therefore I loved the British.

Although I went to almost all movies from 1945 to 1951, I did not like them all. I particularly despised Roy Rogers movies, especially the singing parts. I OD on cowboy and Indian movies. I saw more Indians shot off their horses than there are Indians. Indians and cowboys became as commonplace as the F-curse today.

I loved the exotic, such as the British in India. The storylines were not that different from American Westerns. *The Four Feathers* was my favorite film for many years. It inspired my construction of elaborate battle scenes in my basement using Coca-Cola bottle caps as British and painted green bottle caps as Arabs. Just as in the movies, the British always won.

But loving everything British was not my only contrarian view within my family. As the only one of seven children born in the south—I was born in Miami while my parents were there on a winter vacation—my father sometimes jokingly referred to me as the "cracker," a term for southerners. In films about the Civil War, I sympathized with the Confederates and said as much to my siblings, none of whom agreed with me.

And then there was football. As a predominately Irish-Catholic family, my parents and siblings adored University of Notre Dame. Not me—I always rooted for the University of Michigan football team.

I was not just contrary at an early age, I was also skeptical of authority. I did not always swallow the tales of my elders. Walking my sister Paddy to school one day from our rented house in Miami Springs, in the winter of 1941–42 when I had just turned five years old, there was a cactus bush or tree near the sidewalk. My sister Paddy solemnly told me not to touch the cactus needles because that would kill me. So, of course, I put my index finger on the point of a cactus needle. Nothing happened.

How would a first grader who disliked school respond to the principal who asked the assembled first graders if they *liked* school?

Early on in my first year in first grade, the principal swept majestically into our classroom. We all rose and said in unison, "Good morning, Mother." Don't ask why the principal was called "Mother" because I never knew. She asked us, in her booming, bubbly voice, "Now, how many of you *like* school!" I sat in the first seat in the first row. The whole class vigorously raised one arm in affirmation, except me.

Considering the question, I knew I did not like school. So, I did not raise my arm. The principal and Sister Agnes Leo of course noticed that "in-your-face" discrepancy, and they burst out laughing. Sister Agnes Leo picked me up and swung me around so much that one shoe flew off across the classroom. I retrieved it, humiliated.

Ezra was a neighborhood friend when I was in parochial school. He cried a lot, but I felt protective of him. One day a tough kid beat up Ezra. After learning that, I called that kid a Nazi to his face (Ezra was Jewish). Well, the tough kid was also Jewish. To call a tough Jewish kid a Nazi in 1944 was not a good idea. He immediately beat me up.

One day when Ezra was at my house, he spied a crucifix on the wall. He blurted out "Look at that funny Indian!" I was both shocked and amused, so I burst out laughing. I knew that I shouldn't laugh, but I couldn't help it. It was an amusing sacrilege. I thought that Jesus on the cross was as well-known as Mickey Mouse back then. Every parochial school classroom and every Catholic home had a crucifix on the wall.

During World War II, I learned from the radio and newsreels shown at movie theaters that the Germans and Japanese were our enemies and that the British and Russians were our allies. A year after World War II, I learned at parochial school that the Russians and communists everywhere were our enemies. That happened in 1946–47 when I was in fourth grade. And I believed it.

From 1948 through 1951, my family rented cottages on Lake Huron on the Canadian side in Grand Bend. One game I played with my two oldest nephews, Jimmy and Mike, reflected my love of the French, my fascination with war, and my hatred of communists—as a Catholic kid in parochial school, I learned to hate communism. I recall one Sunday at Mass a visiting priest from Spain delivered the sermon. He shouted, "As a priest reverently raised the host in consecration, communist soldiers sliced off his hands!"

The French were fighting communists in the jungles of Indochina (now Vietnam, Cambodia, Laos, and Thailand) at that time, and I was rooting for the French. There was a long stretch of swampy area with high grass near our summer cottage, and we pretended to be French troops hunting for communists in that swamp. I, of course, was the leader of the French. I was wading in swamp water up to my knees. My younger nephew, Mike, was almost up to his waist in water as we moved along. Mike started to cry.

"Mike! You have got to be tough. We are tracking down communists!" I said with conviction. He sucked it up and kept moving through the water. Years later, it was Mike who was drafted and sent to Vietnam, not me, and not his older brother, Jimmy. Mike survived Vietnam.

On summer weekend afternoons, Grand Bend would sometimes

be flooded with high school aged boys in uniforms resembling the famed British 8th army "Desert Rats." They were Canadian boy scouts in summer camp. I was in awe of their appearance—they even wore berets.

My parents wanted me to attend Catholic Central high school for boys because that is the school all of my male relatives and one brother-in-law had attended. I wanted to attend the Jesuit University of Detroit High School because it had a swim team. But, of course, I attended Catholic Central, a decidedly more laid-back school than the University of Detroit High School.

Catholic Central was famous for having good football teams. Some seniors on the varsity team were offered football scholarships to Big Ten colleges each year. I was eager to continue to play as a lineman in high school as I did in elementary parochial school. Catholic Central had two freshmen football teams: light freshmen (maximum weight, 135 pounds) and heavy freshmen (over 135 pounds). I qualified for the light freshmen.

I was a first-string lineman, and our team won every game. But my first game on that team was a personal humiliation. We were playing the light freshmen of Assumption, a boy's high school in Windsor, Ontario. Like Catholic Central, Assumption was run by the Basilian order of priests. It was a boarding school rumored to be tougher than the Marines. At the beginning of the game, we won the toss, and so Assumption kicked off to us. I was nervous, as is normal for the beginning of our first game. I was praying that the kick would go over my head. But the kick came directly to me. Instead of grabbing it and running, I let it pass to the next line of our team. I was so terrified of failure that I would not grasp for glory. My mother and some of my sisters were watching from the stands—how awful I felt. We won that game in spite of my fear, my cowardice. Aversion to risk has been a feature of my life.

My mother was a very devout Catholic. Whenever any of our birthdays was celebrated, she insisted that we tack on to the end of the Happy Birthday song, this phrase: "May the good Lord bless you/ May the good Lord bless you/ May the good Lord bless and keep you/ Happy birthday to you." I found it depressing that she injected religion into a secular family celebration, but I never said so. What I disliked even more was when she would suggest after dinner that we, the children, kneel down with her in the living room and recite the rosary, a fifteen-minute ordeal. But I never objected. I was an obedient son.

My religious devotion was less than my mother's, but it was present. I did not object when she urged me to become an altar boy in sixth grade, so I did. All through high school, during Lent I would rise early on a weekday morning and attend Mass with my sister Joanie, who was fifteen months older than me. No one pressured me to do that. During Lent in high school, I "gave up" candy and smoking cigarettes, as did Joanie. Because Catholic fasting rules (not inflicted on those younger than twenty-one) were suspended on Sundays, we persuaded ourselves that we could smoke and eat candy on Sundays. I looked forward to Saturday nights during Lent. Emerging from a movie theater or dance after midnight, I would light up.

Saturday was the traditional day for confessions at Catholic churches. Though I hated going to confession and no one insisted on it, I did it out of duty. On laid-back Saturday mornings in high school, I would light up the first cigarette and immediately have guilty thoughts, not about smoking, but about my transgressions of Catholic rules. That would trigger the conviction that I should go to confession that day. I longed for any excuse that would postpone that dreaded event for another week. Much later, as an adult, I came to realize that those guilty thoughts were triggered by smoking on an empty stomach. God was not telling me something, my body was.

When I was a child attending parochial school, each day began with Mass, and I went to Mass on Sunday as well with my family. I heard a lot about heaven. I started thinking a lot about heaven, and my thoughts were uncomfortable yet pleasurable because they did not line up with Catholic visions of the afterlife, yet were filled with material delights.

I was told in sermons and in religious class at Catholic school that we would all experience eternal bliss just looking upon God. To me that would wear thin, perhaps in one or two centuries. It might become boring. Back then there was no one I would like to stare at for eternity, not even Myrna Loy. The Muslim vision of fifty virgins is no better. Would they stay virgins? If so, that is a vision of hellish deprivation. And how about the virgins? How long does No. 47 have to wait for any attention?

Catholic theology paints heaven as a very long, an infinite bore, because it is just like a novel that *begins,* "And they lived happily ever after!" No one has written such a novel because no one would read it. Most educated people have read Dante's *Inferno.* Not *Paradiso,* his book about heaven.

Over my years as a Catholic, I've developed my own version of what heaven *should* be like to hold my interest. I imagine everyone in heaven has perfect recall and compulsively speaks the truth. With no shortage of time—time is infinite in heaven—I would seek out deceased people who have captured my interest. I would question them about events in their life, the choices they made, and their second thoughts on all that, post-death. A leisurely lunch with FDR, Churchill, and Stalin would beat staring at God. I'd seek out Albert Camus and George Orwell. Camus would tell me about the frauds who claimed to be in the French underground in World War II. Orwell could explain why he turned away from communism without becoming a right-wing thug. Senator Joseph McCarthy, unable to prevaricate, would tell me how and why he came up with his infamous lists of communists. I would question the priests to whom I so painfully confessed my trivial descents into impurity. Had they suppressed laughs?

In my imagined improved heaven, the long conversations with those I seek out would not occur in a church pew spoken in whispers, but at an outside table of a Paris bistro. A bottomless bottle of a St.-Émilion Bordeaux wine, and those squat unpretentious bistro wine glasses, plus Perrier with lime. I would drink and talk for hours, but never get wasted; just the pleasant buzz that comes in this vale of tears after two of those small bistro glasses of wine. But I feared that even if there was a heaven, the most interesting people would not be there.

In my imagined improved heaven, sometimes I would also go to the Paris bistro alone with a great book I had never read. To know beforehand what unread books I would love, I would confer with God. He (or She) would remind me of what books I had most loved and say, "Well because you found that one so splendid, you will truly treasure this one." In God I would trust. I am sure He would not push Virginia Woolf or David Ricardo (his prose was rumored to be deadly dull) on me. Even though I never finished anything by Thomas Hardy or Anthony Trollope, if God said I would like one, I would have faith.

In my imagined improved heaven, some mornings I would bike on a sleek red racing bike. All of the hills in heaven would be down. After a long exhilarating ride, I would stop at a bistro and have a baguette with brie, green grapes, and a cold crisp glass of Pinot Grigio. Then home for a nap. This is a better plan for eternity than religion has provided.

Chapter Three

High School

In my freshman year of high school at Catholic Central, my friends were Earl R., Jim W., and Greg S.

Earl had a friend from elementary school who was at U. of D. High, Tom Crimmins, who became one of our group. He was tall, soft spoken, and droll beyond belief for a fourteen-year-old kid. Unlike most teenage boys of that era, Crimmins paid no attention to his appearance: his dress, his shoes, his hair, and most especially his fingernails, announced, to put it kindly, a person who was not fastidious. He was not trying to make a bold, non-conformist statement, rather he did not see the point. He calmly explained this when we, being teenage boys to whom tact with our peers was unknown, would ridicule him for his decidedly uncool appearance.

We hung out after school playing touch football at the U. of Detroit or cards in Earl's basement on cold days. Weekend nights we went to high school sporting events. Although none of us was old enough to drive legally, Crimmins and Earl knew how to drive.

Charlie C., a sometime companion, would stealthily roll his Dad's car down the driveway with the lights and engine off, then start it. We would all go for a ride. Crimmins never took his parents' car. Instead, he would steal stranger's cars for an evening of driving around. He was expert at hot wiring cars. Crimmins never did that with us but with another bolder, friend of his. When the neighborhood newspaper ran an article about a "rash of car thefts," Crimmins was amused, revealing to us that he and his chum were responsible for all of them.

The four of us did a great deal of talking and arguing, especially on the nights we would pay a bowling alley pin boy (none of them was a boy) to buy us beer. One night, Crimmins shocked and appalled us all. It was 1952 and the conversation had turned to the Cold War, and the hot war in Korea. We fervently voiced our jingoish views, nurtured daily by our parents, teachers, the press, and popular shows, such as *I was a Communist for the FBI.* Crimmins would have none of it, arguing that nationalism and all its patriotic claptrap was silly. It was not that he had some idealistic vision of one world at peace, but rather he refused to be bamboozled by propaganda for "our side," knowing that the "other side" used similar propaganda to develop feeling of aggression in their boys. Crimmins was a natural iconoclast. It was not something he aspired to, he simply observed the world, and that was the outcome, at age fourteen. I was agitated for weeks by that conversation. I had never heard such views expressed. What troubled me most was the gnawing thought that he was right, and I had been duped.

Later in high school, when we all drove legally, we became interested in girls. (An anthropologist of the future, writing *Coming of Age in Detroit* will stress the centrality of driving to achieving manhood.) But not Crimmins. Again, with the subtlety of an earth moving machine, we collectively upbraided him for not getting all hot about girls in our private exchanges. As we pounded away with our question, "Why aren't you interested in girls?" he finally blurted out with exasperation. "Oh, they are just like Indians! They like shiny things!" He meant Native Americans, but no one in the 1950s had ever heard of a Native American.

Earl, driving us around in his snazzy car one afternoon, wanted to "pick up" some girls. Crimmins was in the front seat and so he was badgered into making the first pass. Coming along a lone pretty girl walking, Earl slowed down and hissed "OK, Crimmins, try!" In his laconic style Crimmins said, "Hi baby, want a ride?" It didn't work.

Crimmins played the piano, not with great skill but without the annoying tentativeness of so many. Once he started a piece, he plowed on to the end. Crimmins was not fond of the maudlin, cloying popular songs of the 1950s. His tastes ran from Bach to jazz, to simple nineteenth-century American ditties the nuns taught us in elementary school. A booming baritone, he would sing as he pounded out:

"Bill Grogan's goat
Was feeling fine.
Ate three red shirts
From off the line."

Crimmins showed his contempt for a popular song of the day, "Crying in the Chapel," by demonstrating that he could play the whole song by rolling a softball back and forth across the black keys without picking it up.

Upon graduation from high school, Crimmins and I began a less-than-earnest search for summer employment. His father, an accountant with the IRS, got us clerical jobs there dealing with individual tax returns We worked on different floors of the vast IRS bureaucracy. One day I went to visit Crimmins on his floor. He had made the job more interesting for his co-workers by demonstrating that the stiff, narrow W-2 forms they were supposed to check made excellent paper airplanes. Windows were open, and the high-ceilinged room had become a crowded air space with some planes soaring out the windows. Many taxpayers were no doubt puzzled and terrified by stern letters from the IRS demanding that they submit the missing W-2 forms.

Chapter Four

College

When I began college in 1955 at Fordham University, a Jesuit school in New York City, I was unsure of what major to choose. I had a strong desire to *understand* how the world worked. As a freshman at Fordham, one of my required courses was basic economics. And in that course the bells and whistles went off. I believed that now I understood how the world works, and so I chose economics as my major. I have never been sorry that I made that choice.

I completed only one year as a student at Fordham, then transferred to the University of Detroit. My parents were disappointed. The reason I gave was that at Fordham as an economics major, I had to take many business courses that I was not interested in, whereas at the University of Detroit I would have more electives in literature and philosophy. That was partly true but it was a made-up reason. The truth was that I was lonesome and unhappy at Fordham. All of the freshmen in my dorm were business school majors. They were singularly boring, especially my roommate, Ed Walsh. Older than the rest of the freshmen, Ed had enlisted in the Air Force after high school. He was assigned to a U.S. air base in Ireland. In his years in Ireland he amassed a long-playing record collection of 1950s maudlin, popular, Irish music. I had brought my phonograph and jazz albums to college, and I allowed my roommate to play his records too. My punishment for that good deed was listening to that cheery dribble each day. But then something wonderful happened. Ed flunked out after the first semester and returned home to New Jersey. He departed with all his records, and I had the room all to myself! The Jesuit priest assigned to our dorm wrongly assumed that I was unhappy about being alone. I suspect that he persuaded the other boys on our floor to befriend me. So, one weekend afternoon about a half-dozen of them visited me in my room. They were friendly and chatty. One of them asked about the framed picture of my girlfriend back in Detroit.

"Is that your girlfriend?" he asked in a friendly tone.

"No. That's her picture." I replied. He scowled at me, and nobody laughed.

I made one good friend at Fordham: Mike Shea. He was an English major and the most well-read kid I knew. We drank a lot of beer together, usually outdoors. One night we were sitting on a pedestrian bridge over the elevated train that ran up Webster Avenue in the Bronx, drinking beer. After a few beers he said that I was his best friend, I replied the same.

All of my friends from high school went to the University of Detroit for college. Crimmins, Earl, and Jim all began as engineering students, a well-traveled highway for Detroit boys. But after one week in the engineering college, Crimmins quit and became a math major in Arts and Sciences. He was a brilliant math student with no visible effort.

In their senior year, students who majored in math had to pass a one-hour oral exam given by a team of math professors. It was a source of anxiety for the math students, but not for Crimmins. On the day of his exam, I met him in the student union a half hour before his oral exam. He was struggling to remove a plastic coffee cup from his index finger. I suggested that he go in the lavatory and drench his hand in soap and hot water to free the cup from his finger. He did, but no luck. So, at the appointed time he went to his oral exam with the plastic coffee cup dangling from his index finger.

On the main street bordering the campus was a down-scale restaurant called Peter Pan, which all the students called The Pan. It had marvelous deep booths of dark wood. The proprietor, John, and his only employee, Tony, were Greek. John was morose and fretful, while Tony was the opposite. Tony's wonderful hamburgers cost twenty-five cents, as did bottles of local beer. Many of us went there after classes. Crimmins went there every day. Our conversations, coaxed by the twenty-five-cent beers, were often about what we were reading and learning in philosophy courses, which at Jesuit college in the 1950s was limited to Plato, Aristotle (the darling ancient of the Jesuits), Augustine, and of course Thomas Aquinas. Because Tony was Greek, we sometimes questioned him about the ancient era.

Why we thought he might have privileged information can only be ascribed to the beer. But Tony was happy to oblige with ribald anecdotes about ancient Greek men, stories he probably heard from male schoolmates behind the proverbial barn, or its Greek equivalent back in Athens. We never heard such stories in class. They were wonderful antidotes to the solemn pictures of the ancient Greeks painted by our professors.

By the time of our undergraduate days of dallying at The Pan, Crimmins blossomed from a witty nerd to a formidable intellectual iconoclast. Earl R. and Greg S. had other interests. Jim W. and I continued in close association with Crimmins, and the group was joined by a few other male students. That is not to say that Crimmins was the center of that boisterous set of would-be intellectuals. Rather, he was in The Pan every afternoon. If any of us was there, we joined him.

Although I had majored in economics in college, literature was my love. The choice of economics was tied to my middle-class grim conviction that college was the ticket to a comfortable life so long as the education rendered one employable. Of course, accounting or engineering would provide such a ticket, I realized, but those subjects did not grab my intellect as did economics. Other than teaching high school, which would provide a less-than-comfortable life, I could not envision what doors to respectable, well-paid careers are opened by majoring in English. My family was far from poor, but they were educationally challenged. My father had completed high school, my mother had not. All but one of my six older siblings had the briefest encounters with college—from one to three semesters. Their experience of college was closer to a mugging than an epiphany.

I completed college at the University of Detroit, a Jesuit college. None of my close friends chose to major in economics; they were all English or math or physics majors. They good-naturedly ridiculed me for choosing to major in economics, which they considered a branch of business. But I found economics to be intellectually engaging and was never dissuaded by their dismissal of economics as not a serious subject. Because of my love of literature however, I minored in English, and actually published a poem in the college literary magazine. It was imitative of T.S. Eliot, who was all the rage on college campuses back then in the 1950s. Here is the beginning of that poem as I remember it:

I raise the grinning boar
And let it fall on the gray door
Footsteps in the hall
A composure is composed
Taking face from the boar, who approves.

In the middle of my junior year, I fell in love with Brigid, also a University of Detroit undergraduate. She was pretty, vivacious, and smart. Part of her appeal was that she was outspoken and irreverent. In a philosophy class, the professor asked a student to name characteristics of existentialist novels. He named one: numerous characters. Brigid piped up "Oh, then the telephone book qualifies as existentialist!" Another time I took Brigid to a big party my parents had at our house. The wife of one of my cousins buttonholed Brigid and me to tell us about a lecture she had attended by a Catholic mystic woman. "It was so moving!" she gushed. "At the end she raised her arms to the side and said, 'Remember, man is the only animal made in the shape of a cross!'"

Brigid immediately quipped, "And in the shape of a chair."

One summer night in 1958 I went with Brigid and a half-dozen friends down to an exclusive neighborhood on the Detroit River called Greyhaven. One unoccupied house, a marble Italianate mansion, had a magnificent lawn that stretched down to the river. Supplied with much beer, we were inspired to do a scene from *Romeo and Juliet* on the grand porch facing the river. One of our classmates, Pat McNally knew most of the lines. An actor in college plays, he coached Brigid on Juliet's part. He, of course, played Romeo. Pat had entered a Trappist monastery after high school where he stayed in silence for one year. Ever since then, he had been making up for lost time—while awake, he was never silent. His embrace of spirituality did not end with the Trappists. He fled them for a Jesuit seminary where he learned Greek and Latin. A few years there and his thirst for the religious life was cancelled. Acting, partying, and confounding professors with impertinent questions, he then pursued with religious zeal. In a great books class that I also attended, the professor asked Pat to read aloud a passage from Aristotle's *Politics*. Pat breezily announced that his copy was in Greek.

When I was a senior in college, I was determined to go to

graduate school to earn a master's degree in economics. By that time, I proudly considered myself a Fabian Socialist—likely an effect of my Anglophilia, a characteristic that dated from my childhood. It also came from my impression that the Fabians in power in Britain had created a more compassionate state, especially with their nationalized health care.

But before going to graduate school, I was eager to spend a spell in New York.

In January 1959, with one elective short of graduation from college, I moved to New York City, the realization of a dream to live as a bachelor there before settling down in middle class comfort. The first month I was searching for an apartment and a job. I soon learned that with a 1-A draft status, my job prospects were narrow. I wrote to Brigid back in Detroit:

> *I realize that the millstone around my neck, my scarlet letter, has been that ominous and unavoidable fact of my draft status: 1-A. I think that I have described to you the reaction of possible employers upon learning that. It is like being a leper or a carrier of bubonic plague. The caste system has been manifested to me in a most personal manner.*

The intercession of a sympathetic cousin of my mother's enabled me to join an army of clerks at the Home Insurance Company on Wall Street. The work was mind-numbing but not exhausting. The heaviest things I lifted each day were stacks of IBM punch cards.

Most of my clerical co-workers were high school graduates from Brooklyn and the Bronx. They were friendly, funny, and had accents that set my teeth on edge. It was there that I realized that the fabled New York accent of films and TV was a class marker, as was cockney in London. Educated New Yorkers did not sound like that.

I found a studio apartment on West 14th Street, west of 8th Avenue. It was on the first floor in a four-story apartment building. With little difficulty, I persuaded my Fordham friend Mike Shea to abandon dorm living in the Bronx and share the apartment. There was one large window facing 14th Street. The moldings had so many coats of cheap white paint that they disappeared into the walls. Although old, the only fine feature was its fifteen-foot-high ceiling. As an undergraduate at an undistinguished college in Detroit, my dream had been to live in Greenwich Village among writers and artists in a bohemian apartment. The north side of 14th Street was not technically in Greenwich Village, but it was as close as I could afford.

To fulfill my last requirement for graduation, I enrolled in a Chaucer course at the City College of New York, up in Harlem. I learned to read Middle English. Arcane skills in literature were badges of honor bestowing bragging rights in my circle of intellectual undergraduates. As a Catholic intellectual steeped in the Middle Ages, Chaucer was the perfect choice. I selected as my paper for that course a comparison of Chaucer's *Troilus and Cressida* with Shakespeare's. Not surprisingly, I argued, and believed, that Chaucer's version was superior. When the professor read aloud from *The Canterbury Tales* it came alive as lyrical poetry. Pronouncing it correctly unlocked the sonorous beauty, and so I too learned to pronounce Middle English, sometimes reading it aloud when alone.

Some weekday mornings when I felt ambitiously devout, I would rise early and go to Mass before heading down to work in Wall Street. The Catholic church was on 14th Street near 7th Avenue. Walking along the street before 8 a.m., I would see longshoremen in heavy boots with lunch pails and hooks walking west to the Hudson River piers. They were the genuine articles, tough and grizzled. To me, a mid-westerner, longshoremen were as exotic as French Foreign Legionnaires.

One intellectual pursuit I achieved in my New York sojourn, other than the Chaucer course, was a careful study of James Joyce's *Ulysses*. I had read Joyce's *Portrait of the Artist as a Young Man* in college and loved it. It spoke to me as another Irish-Catholic idealist enamored with literature. By the end, the character Stephen Dedalus had abandoned Catholicism. That saddened me, but I was sympathetic to his choice. Some Catholic intellectual had once argued that if you stopped believing you were intellectually duty-bound to leave the Catholic Church.

I read Stuart Gilbert's critical explication of *Ulysses* as well as the *Odyssey*. The Gilbert book was organized around the sequence of chapters in *Ulysses*. I read a chapter in Gilbert, then the corresponding part of the *Odyssey*, and finally the referenced chapter in *Ulysses*. It was work, but I loved it. I realized that I would have missed a great deal in *Ulysses* if I had read it without those aids. Had I not been enamored with the New Criticism of I. A. Richards, all the rage in the 1950s, I simply would have read *Ulysses* as most people read novels—as a pleasant pastime. But it was not just I.A. Richards, it was my Thomistic education at a Jesuit university. That had not made me more spiritual, more into mysticism, but more coldly rational. Understanding, knowing, trumped feeling. That was part of the appeal of economics to me. It was coldly rational, whereas the other social sciences seemed opinionated and touchy-feely.

One Saturday night when I was out alone, I stopped in a bar on Greenwich Avenue, crowded and dark. When I became accustomed to the dim light, I noticed that there were no women in the place. I had never been in a gay bar before and was not sure I was in one now. I had been to the famous McSorley's Old Ale House on East 7th Street where no women were allowed entrance back then. The time I was there, a college boy ordered a Bud at the bar. McSorley's served only their own dark brew, McSorley's ale. The bartender planted his meaty fists on the bar and said, with contempt, "Do you want that with training wheels, sonny?"

Perhaps this was another bar with such a rule, I thought. Looking around, I decided, mistakenly, that I was not in a gay bar. I had always imagined gay bars as drawing flamboyant, effeminate men in bizarre outfits, announcing their homosexuality. None of the patrons matched my ill-informed vision. I was slight, fair, with blond hair almost white, and androgynous features. In some circles I was described as a choir boy. In this circle I was assumed to be one of them. Therefore my presence was not noted as an intrusion by an obviously straight college boy seeking amusement at their expense.

A middle-aged man in a suit and tie began chatting with me at the bar. "I've never seen you here before," he began.

"I'm new to the neighborhood, and in fact new to New York."

"Where do you come from?"

"Detroit."

"A good place to leave."

"And New York is a good place to come to."

"What did you do in Detroit?"

"I was in college, but now I am finished."

"Did you have a boyfriend there?"

"Oh, I had lots of boyfriends." I was clueless. My notion of boyfriends was guys with whom you partied, drank beer, and discussed philosophy, literature, and music. That was not the notion of the middle-aged man, who moved his stool closer.

"I've only one boyfriend at a time," he confided. *How odd and unsocial,* I thought, but I let that remark go by.

"What do you do in New York?" I asked.

"I'm an editor at a university press," he replied.

"Did you major in English in college?" I asked with interest.

"No, I majored in philosophy."

I was duly impressed. "Really! I minored in philosophy, and English too, because I found them so fascinating."

"Where?"

"At a Jesuit college—the University of Detroit."

"I thought they were all named Loyola."

I laughed. "No, there are Georgetown, Fordham, and Boston College that showed some imagination too."

"Was it all Thomistic philosophy there?"

"Oh no, we studied Aristotle and Plato too, plus some moderns like Jacques Maritain and Teilhard de Jardin." Those moderns were all successors to Thomas Aquinas.

"Did you read Plato's accounts of homosexuality in Athens and Sparta?"

"No! Was there much homosexuality in ancient Greece?"

"Oh yes. It's in Plato, other writers, and depicted in some of the extant pottery art."

I was stunned. That had never been mentioned in any of my classes. "Was Plato sympathetic or disapproving of homosexuality?"

"He was matter-of-fact. That's what men did."

I believed back then that the Greek philosophers were precursors of a Christianity that abhorred such perversions, and rightly so I thought. Indeed, I recalled some theological argument that placed Aristotle, Plato, and other pre-Christian great thinkers in heaven without benefit of baptism. I had little sense then of how much like law theology was. Uncomfortable exclusions would be grandfathered in, satisfying current notions of justice. How had I missed the homosexuality? I asked with some tone of skepticism, "Where in Plato is homosexuality discussed?"

"In *The Republic*."

I had read *The Republic*, but then recalled I had read only the assigned parts. Had my Jesuit teachers omitted the parts on homosexuality, and steered their Catholic students to whatever in Plato could be construed as supporting the Christian view of "the good life"? That was dishonest and manipulative, I thought. Of course this was not the first time I found the Church and the Jesuits morally culpable. I did not so much feel the moral indignation of the young, and therefore naive, but rather the shame and consternation of someone who has been sold the Brooklyn Bridge.

By then we had strolled outside together.

"Do you have a boyfriend or boyfriends here in New York?" the man asked. By then I got his true meaning.

"No. I have a girlfriend back in Detroit. We will marry soon." That was meant as a refusal, but the man was persistent.

"You should seek other experiences before you marry. It will broaden your appreciation of the varieties of sexual pleasure."

I was terrified. I was being propositioned by a man. My impulse was to flee, screaming. But instead I said rather stiffly because I was frightened, "I only want the passionate love of the fine woman who loves me. That is more than enough."

"Maybe that seems enough now. But maybe your Jesuits have trapped you, closeted you, in a vanished world. Here you are in New York City in 1959 with fabulous opportunities for new erotic experiences, and you shut them off. The world has changed. Your Scholastic philosophers are dead. Forgotten. They have nothing to say to us."

"Oh, I think they still do." I said lamely. We shook hands and parted. Walking home, I had uncomfortable thoughts. My education in philosophy was limited to the Scholastic philosophers and their Greek predecessors, then jumping to the modern Christian existentialists. I was determined to correct this enormous omission in my education, starting with *all* of Plato's *Republic* to see if he praised homosexuality, or simply shrugged it off as what men do. I hoped that neither was the case. That is probably why I postponed that intellectual quest.

Brigid visited me in New York in February, and stayed at the Chelsea Hotel on West 23rd Street. She had been in New York once before as a child with her parents. I took her around to many of the sites. On her last night in New York we saw the off-Broadway play, *Abelard and Heloise.* The succumbing of the two characters to Eros was duly punished. Abelard was castrated and Heloise committed to a convent. Their transcendence to a lifelong chaste agape was a magnificent spiritual triumph preserved in their years of correspondence. For me back then it was a happy ending. Brigid said it was depressing. She was right.

One spring night after class as I started down Convent Avenue, I caught a view across the Hudson River of the Palisades Amusement Park brilliantly illuminated. The Ferris wheel was silhouetted against the dark sky. I suddenly recalled the previous spring at an amusement park with Brigid when we first expressed, in words, our undying love. It was on a Ferris wheel. Rapture recalled. I was so happy. We were determined to be married. Less permanent options to sate my lust—a characterization of my love at which I would have taken umbrage—I rejected. The not-so-hidden injuries of a Catholic education. I told myself that my exquisite longing was driven by agape, not Eros.

Chapter Five

Army Life

In early June 1959, I gave up my 14th Street apartment and returned to Detroit for my college graduation. Immediately after that I reported to the army for my six months of service, an option preferable to the two years of service if I waited for the inevitable draft call.

I went through basic training at Fort Leonard Wood in Missouri, south of St. Louis. My company of thirty or so recruits was assigned to a barracks and introduced to our officer for the next eight weeks. Crisp, starched, pressed, always wearing sunglasses and carrying a riding crop, the tall black lieutenant always led us in the morning runs. The other companies of recruits were just emerging from their barracks as we ran by singing. Whatever physically grueling tasks we were required to do, he did too. On the way to the mess hall before each meal, he had us go single-file up to a chinning bar and do three pullups. I was able to do that. Those who couldn't do three, he would make do three pushups instead. For those who didn't do the pullups right, he would demonstrate how to do them. Thus, he probably did a dozen or more himself before each meal. One southern white boy, large and obese, would hang from the bar hopelessly struggling to do one pullup, his massive body shaking all over. He never made it up. So, the lieutenant commanded him to do ten pushups, a number he never achieved. The lieutenant ignored that second public failure. Lazy, unkempt, obese, the southern boy was everything the lieutenant was not. And because he was white, he came to hate the lieutenant for all those unfavorable contrasts. During rigorous field exercises in the July heat of southern Missouri, the southern boy would sweat and pant far more than the rest of us. Blaming the lieutenant, he would hiss under his breath "Goddamn nigger!" Once the lieutenant certainly must have heard him, but he majestically ignored it. Would Adonis retaliate against a bloated toad? Years later when I saw the scene in the film *Full Metal Jacket* when the recruit blew his hated sergeant away in a men's room, I remembered the southern boy. I thought that if the southern boy had the chance he would have done the same to our lean black lieutenant.

The army gave me a choice of specialization, post basic training: infantry, artillery, or medics. With the speed of light I made my choice: medics. Although I made that choice for physical safety, it was the right choice for comradery. Almost all of my fellow medic trainees with whom I lived for four months were college graduates. Many, but not all of them, were smart, articulate, and witty. Two singularly foul-mouthed boys from New Jersey were voluble. In their incessant banter one once said to the other, "You bought a second-fucking-hand car? You idiot!"

One of my Ivy League medic trainees quipped, "I have heard many variations on 'fuck;' a verb, a noun, an adverb; but this is the first time I have heard it used as a hyphen!"

My favorite in our group of thirty or so going through medic training was a tall redhead, Leon. He was a Columbia College graduate. The fact that Leon had been in a class taught by Jacques Barzun was reason enough for me to like him. I had recently read Barzun's *The House of Intellect.* It meshed with my rational, intellectual, elitist disdain at the time for modern America, and it reinforced my attraction to economics as a coldly rational pursuit.

Leon told me that he was awarded the Phi Beta Kappa key at graduation. On his return home to St. Louis after graduation, he tossed his Phi Beta Kappa key from a bridge into the Mississippi River—another iconoclast. His family was Jewish but non-devout; some of his relatives were devout Jews. When he was about ten years old one of those relatives, an aunt, was a guest for dinner at his home. He told me that he surreptitiously added some non-kosher food—disguised bacon—to her plate. He claimed he did that out of curiosity, not malice. Wondering what might happen once she had eaten it all, as he suspected, nothing happened. Then he announced to all at the dinner table, "I put bacon in your dish." She looked shocked, as did the others. His father was angry and sent him away from the table.

There was another mate in my barracks of medics in training

at an army base in San Antonio that I was fond of. He was an Ivy League graduate and asked me to take his place for weekend guard duty, a rotating chore. "I have been so eager to go to a whore house in Mexico this weekend Matt, would you please take my place for guard duty?"

"Sure," I replied, happy to help him out. So, he went to the brothel that weekend, and I covered his guard duty. When I told Brigid on the phone of the generous act I had done for a friend, she said, "You enabled him to fornicate, which is certainly a sin." I had not thought of that, but I agreed that she was right. The next time I went to confession at the Catholic chapel on the base, I told the priest what I had done. He agreed that it was a sin, and I felt ashamed. In retrospect, I think I did the right thing in enabling him to go to the brothel. Fornication is not adultery. The Catholic prohibition of fornication is as arbitrary as their fasting rules, that they have now abolished. Maybe before effective birth control, the rule was sensible. It makes no sense now.

Later, that friend related to me how uncomfortable the prostitute made him feel. "Her room had a crucifix on the wall, and a picture of the Virgin Mary. How hypocritical!" he said indignantly. I immediately disagreed but kept that to myself. I think that prostitution is never a happy choice but a desperate choice for survival. Let her have her symbols of piety.

In early December, my six months of active duty in the army ended. I flew home to Detroit from San Antonio. On the plane ride I had an unforgettable dream. In it, the plane crashed on an airport runway. I was lying on my back outside the burning plane near death. A friend from college who had a crush on Brigid, Jim, suddenly appeared and whispered to me "I will die in your place."

Chapter Six

Marriage, University of Michigan, and a Move to New York

In February 1960, I married Brigid in a Catholic church. We had agreed beforehand that I would attend graduate school full-time beginning in the autumn.

We also agreed to practice the "rhythm" method of birth control, the only method endorsed by the Church. Because of the forthcoming Vatican II conference called by the seemingly liberal pope, John XXIII, we had high hopes that the recently introduced birth control pill would be approved for use by Catholics. Our hopes were dashed.

The rhythm method of birth control did not work for us. Brigid became pregnant in the spring semester of my full-time graduate studies. Sometime after our son, Matt Jr. was born in November 1961, Brigid persuaded me that she should go on the pill because it was effective. Then she stopped going to Sunday Mass with me. I asked her why and she replied, "I can no longer be a Catholic because it requires obeying their rules on birth control, and I no longer do." That saddened me, but I was impressed with her principled choice. I continued to be a practicing Catholic while rejecting the Church's stand on birth control. Hypocrisy? Maybe. But my choice was typically American, just like in the saying: "The English obey all laws, the French obey no laws, and the Americans only obey the convenient laws."

In the autumn of 1960, I began my graduate studies in economics at the University of Michigan, the same year that John F. Kennedy ran against Richard Nixon to become president. In the macroeconomics course I took that semester, students asked the professor, Gardner Ackley, how he thought the Michigan economics faculty would vote. He replied that probably all but four of the faculty of around twenty-eight would vote for Kennedy. It pleased me to hear that the faculty was mostly Democrats, as was I. That was before the big shift to the right by economists beginning in the 1970s.

As a graduate student at Michigan, I was disabused of my Fabian Socialist views and became a neoclassical economist. That was because my professors convinced me that socialism was always a bad idea, pointing out that living standards in Eastern Europe, satellites of the Soviet Union, were far below ours. We did not hear about the success of democratic socialism in Scandinavian nations. I had some wonderful professors at Michigan: Gardner Ackley, who was later appointed to Kennedy's Council of Economic Advisors, and eventually under President Johnson became the head economist of the Council; Daniel Suits, a statistics whiz who developed one of the first econometric models of the U.S. economy; and the famous Kenneth Boulding, author of *Economic Analysis*, a basic economics text book for colleges. That book included a cogent summary of what was called the Neoclassical-Keynesian synthesis, a merging of Keynesian macroeconomics with neoclassical economics (that synthesis was mostly rejected by mainstream economists in the 1970s as they moved away from Keynesian thought).

Boulding was notorious around campus for his daily silent protest. As a Quaker, he was strongly opposed to the United States growing involvement in the Vietnam conflict. Each class day at noon he would stand in silent protest in the middle of the grassy quad as thousands of students milled about. Another one of my professors at Michigan was George Katona, the psychologist who founded the Survey Research Center at Michigan that became the model for the federal government's establishment of a monthly consumer survey that is still in operation.

In the spring of 1961, at the end of my one-year master's program in economics, I had not yet graduated because I had not completed my master's thesis. There was a national recession and Detroit was hit very hard. Who needs an economist in a recession? Brigid and I decided that I would go alone to New York to find work, and then we would move there. My sister Joanie and two friends shared a rent-controlled apartment on East 87th Street. I would stay with her while searching for a job.

So this unemployed economist, with a pregnant wife, moved to the Big Apple.

Chapter Seven

Corporate Economist at General Motors

That autumn I ended up employed as a junior economist at General Motors in New York. The irony of that was evident to me. The General Motors headquarters was in Detroit, and it was the largest private sector employer in that city back then. The corporation's president was located in Detroit. The chairman and the treasurer's office were in New York. The economics department was in Detroit and focused on the automobile industry.

The treasurer's office in New York had a small economics section that focused on everything else: macroeconomics, finance, and international trade. This was a great learning experience for me, even though I had no desire to become an expert on the economy of automobiles. When I studied macroeconomics at Michigan, all of the definitions of the national income accounts went in one ear and out the other. But at GM I had to *know* them in order to write coherent and lucid reports on the national economy.

Work at GM in the 1960s was, unfortunately, not all learning to be a competent macroeconomist. When the retired long-time chairman of GM, Alfred Sloan, wrote his book, *My Years with General Motors*, we in the economics office were drafted as fact checkers of his text before publication. No fact was too trivial to be checked, and the book had a lot of facts. Cold war paranoia was alive and well in the corridors of GM. In 1962, shortly after Castro came to power in Cuba, we were offered bumper stickers that proclaimed, "Don't Worry They Are Only 90 Miles Away!"

The chief of the corporate economists was Brec Micoleau. He was wise, taciturn, and old fashioned. He used a slide rule for all his calculations, while the rest of us had Monroe calculators, as big and heavy as typewriters—it was the era before hand-held calculators and desk top computers. He had a small staff: an assistant chief and three economists, including me.

His assistant chief, Bob Godridge, was enthusiastic and hard-working. Brec often chided him for his late hours. "You know Bob, eighty percent of a solution to any problem is uncovered in the first twenty percent of time spent." But Bob nevertheless would forge ahead late at night to discover the solution.

I was fond of Bob. His enthusiasm was infectious. Not just about macroeconomic problems, but also about the culture of General Motors. "If the top forty men [it was always men] of GM suddenly died in a plane crash, their underlings would be ready to replace them!" he bragged to us at lunch one day. I thought that was a bad policy: overstaffing. But I said nothing. Bob also bragged about GM's solid financial rules. Ready cash and liquid securities should always be high. That rule was established by Alfred Sloan when he was sent from DuPont to rescue GM in the early 1920s. A severe cash crunch almost wiped out GM back then. Never again.

Pay and bonuses for the top tier of management at GM were beyond generous for that era. Each year, publicly listed corporations are required to show the salary and bonus of the highest-ranking executives in their 10-K reports to the Securities and Exchange Commission. The 10-K reports must be released to the public. Bob boasted, "The GM executives were always at the top of the list for compensation among the largest corporations, and in fact some GM executives whose compensation did *not* require listing outranked the pay and bonuses of many chief executives at other corporations!" The reason Bob knew that was because his friends in the much larger treasurer's department of GM told him.

Hugh Lynch was hired for our small section a few months after I was. No one told me about that beforehand, so I was nervous that he was there to soon replace me. That was not the case. Hugh and I became friends and we often had lunch together. One warm spring day in 1962, Hugh and I were strolling along West 57th Street when he remarked how delightful it was to see pretty girls in sexy spring outfits that emphasized their full breasts. He inferred happily that their outfits signaled that they were available for intimacy. I froze, making no comment. I only spoke to my wife about sex and that rarely. He must have sensed my aversion to that topic because he never raised it again with me. He probably thought me a prude, and he was right.

Hugh enlightened me about the rigid class system in New York. Growing up on the west side of Detroit, I thought in high school that we Irish Catholics were at the top of the heap, whereas Polish and Black people were at the bottom. In my Jesuit college everyone was Catholic, but some of them from the east side had WASP friends who attended Ivy League schools. To me, those WASPs ranked higher than we Irish Catholics.

Hugh taught me differently about Irish Catholics in New York. He said, "My first job after getting my MBA at NYU was with one of the big banks of New York. There were two training programs, one for guys with Ivy League degrees from well-to-do families, and one for everybody else. For guys in the first group, the sky was the limit for how high they could rise in the bank. For guys like me in the second group, the highest we could rise was to become a branch manager. So I quit and came to GM."

I had read about the anti-Irish past of New York, when help-wanted newspaper ads sometimes noted "No Irish need apply," but I thought that was long ago. While I searched for work in the summer of 1961, I sometimes saw help-wanted ads for college graduates that ended "Out-of-town degree required." When I asked Hugh to enlighten me about that, he said, "They want to exclude City College of New York graduates, mostly Jewish, and all the Catholics from Fordham, St. Johns, and other small Catholic colleges in the city."

Every holiday season, GM held a Christmas party at a fancy hotel on Central Park South. I attended each one them in the three years I worked there. Spouses were invited and some did attend. There was a lot of good food and much drinking. Many secretaries (all women) departed with tipsy executives (all men). In recent years I have seen a few episodes of the television hit *Mad Men*. My wife was taken with the show. I was not. "Why don't you like it?" she asked me.

"Because I lived through it in 1960s corporate America," I replied.

In those years, the early 1960s, GM always ranked first in the Fortune 500 list of public corporations. Back then the Fortune 500 list was limited to manufacturing and mining corporations. Now it includes public utilities, such as AT&T, and giant retailers, such as Walmart, financial firms, and health firms. In the 2018 Fortune 500 list Walmart was first, Exxon Mobil second, Berkshire Hathaway third, and Apple was fourth.

GM ranked tenth—how the mighty have fallen. GM is an oligopoly that was over-staffed and overpaid the top tier of management. It was not prepared for the lowering of trade barriers and the dramatic drop in international shipping costs. Competitors in Japan and Europe have cut deeply into its domestic market.

I left GM near the end of 1964. Why did I quit? For one thing, I realized that as a corporate economist I would not get to choose the economic issues I researched and wrote about. That would be decided by higher-ups. So I needed to get a Ph.D. in economics and become an academic economist. When I was at the University of Michigan, I thought that being a corporate or government economist would be fine, and that a master's degree would be sufficient to pursue that goal. But my time at GM taught me that I was mistaken.

There was also a more immediate cause of my departure. Bob

Godridge, my boss at GM, was promoted and transferred to the Detroit headquarters. His replacement, John Foster, had an MBA from NYU and also worked for GM on the same floor that I did. He was not part of our economics department, but I knew him. Now, as Bob Godridge's replacement, he was my boss, I quickly discovered that he was not qualified for his job. When he was assigned some task by Brec, the economics section head, John would come to me for advice about how to pursue it, but he kept his consultation with me secret from Brec. Thus, I knew he was unqualified, but Brec probably did not. I never told Brec. I thought that I was more qualified than John and should have been made Bob Godridge's successor. But I had been employed there less than two years and was probably five or more years younger than John. GM, I realized, was bureaucratic.

Lastly, and really important, was that my wife, Brigid, urged me to pursue a Ph.D. in economics as a full-time student. I think she realized that I was unhappy there, although I did not complain to her. I was not *aware* of being unhappy at GM until John replaced Bob Godridge. Brigid said that she would expand her private tutoring to support our family of three so that I could go back to graduate school. I jumped at her offer.

General Motors was generous in my departure. They wanted me to come back after I had completed my Ph.D. My family health insurance was continued at GM's expense all through my years as a Ph.D. graduate student at NYU.

Chapter Eight

Ph.D. Student

I began my full-time Ph.D. studies in economics at NYU in the fall of 1965. One required course for all was the history of economic thought. I do not think any graduate programs in economics now have such a requirement. That is unfortunate for the students, as is the disappearance of any economic history requirement.

New York University had an economic history requirement, either European or American—I opted for European. As I noted, I had become a convinced neoclassical economist at the University of Michigan. My professors at NYU were not as engaging as my professors at Michigan. Peter Albin, only slightly older than myself, taught me public finance and the theory of risk and investment. He became my mentor while I was still taking courses and I participated in one of his consulting jobs. His lectures were the source of my awe for the theorists Paul Samuelson, Kenneth Arrow, and Gérard Debreu. Under his influence my neoclassical roots became strengthened, and

I became convinced that neoclassical economics and progressive politics were compatible.

Another of my professors at NYU was not progressive. Israel Kirzner, was a disciple of the right-wing Ludwig von Mises, who was a professor at the NYU business school. Kirzner taught the required microeconomics course. Daniel Khazzoom taught me econometrics. Solomon Fabricant was a noted institutional economist who was a member of the National Bureau of Economic Research (NBER). At that time the NBER was the headquarters of institutional economics and its office was in New York. Fabricant taught me how to write as an economist, purging my purple prose from the many papers I had to write for his course.

Keynesian macroeconomics was still dominant when I was a graduate student at NYU. The young English professor who taught it was engaging, witty, and a strong admirer of Keynes. I studied mathematical economics, all the rage back then as now, under the Japanese professor Taro Yamane. Our text for that course was the manuscript for his forthcoming book. In the last year of my course-work at NYU, I took urban economics, and became hooked forever, not because of the professor who taught it but because of the major readings assigned. And because I had always loved the cities I lived in, Detroit and New York.

Ever since first moving to New York in 1961, we lived in Inwood, the upper Manhattan neighborhood. We were there all through my graduate student years, 1965 to1968. It was the last stop of the west side A train, convenient for first commuting to General

Motors and then to NYU. At the time Inwood was mostly Jewish and Irish-American. Manhattan was far from integrated. Riding home in the evening on the A train, I mused that there might as well be a sign noting "The next stop is 168th Street. All African Americans and Hispanics must get off the train."

While living in Inwood, my son, Matt Jr., began to attend school—the ungraded Montessori school near the U.N. building was the first, and the Cathedral School of St. John the Divine was the second. I think he started there in fourth grade while I was a graduate student at NYU. Each day, I would walk him from our apartment to the No. 1 subway stop at Broadway and 218th Street. He would ride alone down to Broadway and 110th Street, one block from that school, and reverse the trip to return home in the afternoon. The school was famous for its boys choir (no girls were allowed back then). He was not in the choir because of the large time commitment required, but music was a key component of the school.

He told us that students sang "grace" every day at lunch time. "Sing it for us," we asked. Here is what he sang: "For health and strength and deli bread / we praise thy name oh Lord. Amen."

A forgivable mistake for a New York kid.

Here is another one. The students were taught to recite the Lord's Prayer. He got it all right when we asked him to recite it, except for the second-to-last line: "And lead us not into Penn Station/ But deliver us from evil. Amen." Not as bad as leading unaccompanied children into the Port Authority Bus Terminal back then, the late 1960s, but still dangerous.

One of Matt Jr.'s school assignments was to write a letter to any two famous authors. He chose Jacques Cousteau, the ocean naturalist and adventurer, and E. B. White, the author of *Charlotte's Web.* Jacques Cousteau never answered his letter, but E. B. White did. As a doting parent, my esteem for Jacques Cousteau sank while my esteem for E. B White soared.

In 1967, Dick Netzer, then a professor in the economics department, chose me, a graduate student, to be on his Ford Foundation grant. I had been recommended to him by Professor Khazzoom, my econometrics professor. When I went to be interviewed by Netzer, I was nervous, fearing I might not be chosen. In the interview he described the research project, and I became excited because it was an urban economics project. At the end of his explanation I asked, "When will I know if I have been selected for this grant?"

He laughed and replied, "Oh you already have been selected. Do you accept?"

"Yes!" This provided me with full tuition, a stipend for two years, plus a dissertation topic. Before that I had been paying my own way with my wife's and my own tutoring, loans, and occasional consulting. Life became more secure.

Netzer was not a warm and fuzzy person, nor a hands-on taskmaster on the Ford Foundation grant. All of my work under the grant was focused on my dissertation topic: reading, assembling data on three hundred suburban jurisdictions, and testing a myriad of econometric equations. There were three other graduate students supported on the grant. One was another economics graduate student, smart and hardworking. The other two were Graduate Public Administration (GPA) graduate students, now called the Wagner School. They were lazy, incompetent, and clueless as to how to attack the research questions. Their example of how *not* to do social science research made me thankful that I was in economics, not planning or public administration. I became contemptuous of them and their fields. I spent as little time as possible in the office that the four of us graduate students shared. The two GPA graduate students chatted all day, but never about the research topics. That was one distraction of trying to work there.

The other was Simon Goldstein, the future Director of Doctoral Studies, despite his lack of any graduate degrees. Goldstein had the neighboring office and never closed the door when he was in. He talked incessantly on the phone or to visitors. It became clear to me through the number, the length, and the trivial content of those conversations, that Simon did nothing all day.

In the spring of 1968, as student protests over the Vietnam War spread across college campuses, one of the GPA graduate students in our shared office mounted a huge poster of a Columbia student in a bloody ripped shirt, fist raised in defiance. I was indifferent to all of its symbolism. Although I was opposed to the Vietnam War, I had a wife and a son and thus was not drawn into the student revolt. My dreams did not include overthrowing the establishment. Rather, I sought single mindedly a place in the establishment as an intellectual, an academic. And Netzer gave me what I wanted—eventually.

My dissertation topic was an outgrowth of the Ford Foundation grant project. An urban economist at the University of Washington in Seattle, Charles Tiebout argued in a 1956 article ("A Pure Theory of Local Expenditures") that when people choose a home they consider a number of factors other than the physical house and asking price. They might reject one jurisdiction for another—the issue of "voice" or "exit" as it is known in economics and political science. But before Tiebout, it seems no social science writer applied that concept to the myriad suburban jurisdictions surrounding a large city.

I hypothesized that the choice of a suburban jurisdiction in purchasing a home was positively correlated with the quality of public schools there, in addition to factors such as distance to Manhattan and house prices. I assembled a staggering amount of data on three hundred or so suburban jurisdictions around New York City in three states: New York, New Jersey, and Connecticut. And I was planning to do an econometric analysis.

However, my research fellowship expired in June of 1968, before I could complete my dissertation, so I had to seek full-time work. My wife was worn out by long days, heavier on the weekends, of tutoring high school kids in math. Her health and her mental state were deteriorating. I had selfishly overlooked that as I pushed to finish my dissertation as a full-time student, a push that did not succeed. By the winter and spring of 1968 I was alarmed by her condition, and finally realized that I must take over the full financial support of our household. I found a job as a corporate economist with a multinational corporation headquartered in Wall Street, W. R. Grace. I planned to finish writing my dissertation at night and on weekends.

Chapter Nine

W. R. Grace

Although W. R. Grace was a publicly listed corporation, it was controlled by the Grace family, meaning Peter Grace, the chairman and president at that time. Two of his children in their twenties were employed there; headquarters were in the Wall Street area. Peter was addicted to buying existing firms in various industries.

The original W. R. Grace was a shipping firm founded by William Russell Grace, an adventurous Irishman who went to sea in his teens. According to legend around the Grace headquarters where I worked, his original venture was to lease a ship, sail to Peru, purchase a shipload of iguana (bird shit) a popular fertilizer, and sell it in the United States. The firm he leased the ship from refused to take it back because of its awful smell, and so he had to buy the ship. That was the beginning of W. R. Grace as a shipping company. I have found no support for that legend.

William R. Grace thrived. He was elected mayor of New York

City twice in the Gilded Age: 1881–82 and 1885–86. He was the grandfather of Peter Grace.

The corporation W. R. Grace expanded, especially under Peter Grace, into a conglomerate. It was in banking, chemicals, a sporting goods retail chain, a restaurant chain, chocolate, and shrimp processing, to name the ones I remember. Peter created the W. R. Grace economics department at the Wall Street office where I was employed for three years, 1968 to 1971, and then continued as an economic consultant for about nine more years, 1972 to 1979. He used the economics department to explore possible firms to take over. He also used us to beat up on the many subsidiaries that he was unhappy with. We were not well loved in the corporation, except by Peter. He was a numbers freak, and we produced the many reports full of mind-numbing data that he required.

My job at W. R. Grace was to develop econometric models for forecasting commodity prices—sugar, cocoa, palm oil, shrimp, and beef. I was good at it, meaning my forecasts were not wildly off the mark, and I enjoyed it. My boss, David Elkin, had an ABD (all but dissertation) in economics from the New School University in New York City. David's dissertation advisor at The New School was the only remaining neoclassical mainstream economist on the faculty. He was from a family of radical Jewish immigrants and grew up in the Bronx. He told me that in the 1930s and 1940s, "I thought that the Democratic party was the extreme right wing of American politics. I had never heard of Republicans."

Although I was a mainstream neoclassical economist, I was a

political liberal and a proud Democrat. When Nixon was elected president in November 1968, I began wearing a black necktie to my office at W. R. Grace each day. When David asked, "What are you mourning?" I replied simply, "The election of Nixon."

As a progressive Democrat, I was pleased to learn in my first year at W. R. Grace, 1968, that President Kennedy had appointed Peter Grace to head his newly created Alliance for Progress, which had as its aim economic development assistance for Latin America. So I assumed that my CEO was politically progressive, a false assumption I was told by my boss, David Elkin, and later reinforced by Peter's public acts.

One event during my Wall Street sojourn brought home to me how simplistic and silly were the radical stereotypes of American society. I marched in an anti-Vietnam War demonstration in Wall Street. The marchers were mostly smartly dressed men—bankers, stockbrokers, and corporate executives. The numerous loud hecklers were mostly construction workers, clerical workers, and floor clerks from the stock and commodity exchanges in their blue smocks—the working class who bore the tragic brunt of the war.

Chapter Ten

Putnam Valley

After my first year at W. R. Grace, we moved from our Inwood apartment at the northern end of Manhattan to a rented house in Putnam county in 1969. It was deep in the forest on fifty acres. One could walk to the Appalachian Trail from our house without seeing any other residence. My son and wife loved it. They both evolved into avid birders and nature lovers living in Putnam Valley. However, my commute was a grueling two hours: driving to the train station, train to Grand Central, subway to Wall Street.

My son had become a voracious reader even before we lived in Putnam Valley. But while there I would sometimes read him selections from the Bible. A Bible story about a man on a journey who meets and mates a prostitute lead to his asking me this question: "What's a prostitute?" I explained. Thanks to his progressive parents, he already knew how babies were made but did not know about prostitutes. "Who gets the baby if there is one?" was his next question.

"Oh, she does of course," I replied.

"And *he* pays *her*!" He said indignantly. As an economist, I immediately saw the flaw in his expression of outrage. My son's mistake was that he thought, as a prepubescent male, that procreation was the sole purpose of sexual intercourse. Thus, the win-win of free exchange was not evident to him. What did the man get for his payment? It pleased me at the time that he was intuitively predisposed to think like an economist.

It was in Putnam Valley that Brigid became pregnant with our daughter Maureen. And before Maureen's first birthday, her independent spirit was manifested to us. One long weekend my wife, Brigid, and I took our son, Matt Jr., to hike to the top of Mt. Washington in New Hampshire. We hired a teenage girl, the daughter of a friend, to stay with Maureen. While in New Hampshire, one night we stayed in the hotel in Bretton Woods where the World Bank and International Monetary Fund (IMF) were established at an international conference in 1944. John Maynard Keynes, the economic architect of those two institutions, was at that conference. He was my hero for many years.

When we returned home Sunday evening, the babysitter was in tears. "Maureen won't eat! Whenever I try to stick the spoon in her mouth, she won't take it," she cried. We paid her and I drove her home. Brigid was determined to break Maureen's resistance to being fed.

"I will show her who is boss around here!" Brigid hissed. But after one day of determined but futile efforts by Brigid, Maureen showed us. She would only eat if she did the feeding. Never again would someone stick a spoon in her mouth. So we had to come up with food she could manage to steer into her mouth unassisted: bland sausages cut into bite-size pieces easily picked up by a ten-month-old, bananas, and messiest of all, fruit yogurt. Maureen would eagerly take the spoon and shovel the dripping yogurt into her mouth, onto her face, into her hair, and all over her bib. Watching her eat would curb anyone's appetite.

When we first brought Maureen home from the hospital, our neighbor and friend, John Cohen came by. He looked at Maureen and said, "You know I have two children of my own, but that is the most beautiful baby I have ever seen."

I first met John Cohen the day I heard a chain saw buzzing in the woods near our house. I went to investigate, fearing that someone was cutting down our landlord's trees. But no, he was cutting up trees that already had fallen to use for firewood. I was relieved, and John was very affable. We ended up agreeing that we would cut up dead trees, together. He would provide the chain saw and I would provide extra hands to lug all the wood to our homes. I learned that he was a musician, a guitarist, and singer. His music group, the New Lost City Ramblers, was unknown to me but was a popular folk music band. His wife was Pete Seeger's daughter. Later I learned that he was also a documentary film maker and awarded grants from the New York State Arts Council to do movies tied to the history of country music. He had earned an MFA from Yale. One of his films was about some isolated tribe in South America that he befriended. He lived with them for many months and recorded their distinctive music.

John was a true Renaissance man. He taught drawing at one of the State University of New York campuses near Putnam Valley. At his memorial service (John died in 2019), one of the heads of the Smithsonian Institute in Washington delivered a eulogy elaborating on much of John's scholarly work on folk music.

Putnam Valley was only about fifty miles north of New York City, but the winter there was more like the Snowbelt of Buffalo and Rochester. That, in part, was due to its much higher elevation of almost 2,000 feet. We built a short toboggan run down a hill in our front yard and I bought us all snow shoes for hiking in the winter.

Chapter Eleven

Becoming an Assistant Professor

In 1969, the undergraduate School of Commerce at NYU offered me an adjunct position teaching basic economics, which I accepted. The class was at night, and on my way to class one evening I ran into Simon Goldstein, the professor who chatted all day. He told me that Dick Netzer, my dissertation advisor, had been made Dean of the Graduate School of Public Administration at NYU. When Netzer became dean, he brought along Simon to be on the GPA faculty.

It was a fortuitous meeting. Simon said, "Matt! Today at a faculty meeting we voted to require a statistics course for all of our graduate students. We have no one to teach it. You would be perfect! I will speak to the Dean."

So I was hired as an adjunct to teach two sections of basic statistics beginning the next fall term. Luckily for me, I turned out to be good at it. Even more luckily, the dean's secretary, a part-time student in the program (most of the graduate students were part-time), was enrolled in one of my sections that fall. A bright, energetic young woman, she enjoyed the course and did well. I suspect that she conveyed her enthusiasm to the dean.

In the spring of 1971, after I had completed my dissertation and successfully defended it, Dean Netzer offered me a tenure track position to teach the required courses in economics and statistics to the graduate students in the college. The pay was thirty percent below that of my corporate economist job at W. R. Grace, but I jumped at it because my ambition since entering a Ph.D. program in economics was a career as an academic economist. The NYU job was not my ideal because it was not in an economics department. I had an opportunity to be hired by the economics department of the State University of New York at Plattsburgh, but I did not pursue it because Plattsburgh, being far north of Albany and about one hundred miles south of Montreal, had massive snowstorms and bitter cold in the winter there.

I did not want to move my young family to Plattsburgh. So I took the NYU job, thinking that it might be a springboard for a later move to an economics department.

Chapter Twelve

The Faculty Meeting, September, 1971

In early September, 1971, I dressed carefully in my tweed jacket, charcoal gray trousers, white button-down shirt and best necktie, I rushed from my home in Putnam Valley to my first faculty meeting in the Graduate School of Public Administration (GPA) of New York University, now the Wagner School. I was a freshly minted Ph.D. in economics from that university's economics department. As I raced into the grand federal period townhouse, the home of that school, I ran into the dean, Dick Netzer. He was engaged in animated conversation with a senior faculty member.

I smiled and he nodded recognition, and said, "Oh, Perry, this is Matt Drennan, our new hire who will teach the statistics course requirements. Perry shook my hand and asked, "Are you an economist?" When I affirmed that, he frowned.

I was not surprised. A year or two before, Harvard appointed a renowned urban economist to chair the urban planning department in the Graduate School of Design. Because it was Harvard and because their urban planning department was the oldest in the nation, universities with urban planning departments took notice. So when NYU appointed the economist Dick Netzer to be dean of GPA, which included urban planning, health, and public administration, it did not seem unusual. After Netzer's appointment as dean, in addition to me he added two other economists to GPA's faculty of thirty.

I realized that in a department of mostly urban planning and political science professors I would face hostility because of my Ph.D. in economics. Other social scientists were often intimidated by economists because of the mathematical and statistical bent of the profession. More important, however, is the imperial arrogance of so many economists, as Dean Netzer personified.

I knew that if I parroted him, my chances of winning tenure would be near zero. So I determined to keep my head down and to keep some of my strong opinions typical of young neoclassical economists to myself. For example, I viewed urban planning with contempt because of its fundamental premise that cities could be improved by regulation. The market could fix all problems I believed then. No need for politicians to make problems worse.

That morning we all went up the long, plush, carpeted staircase to the conference room on the second floor. Paneled in dark wood, windowless, and dominated by a magnificent mahogany table that would seat twenty or thirty people, the room was lit by a large crystal chandelier hanging from the fourteen-foot, soft white plaster ceiling. I was impressed. The seats were full with men, and a few women, most unknown to me. They looked serious, dignified, and thoughtful. I felt intimidated by the august scene as I took a seat. The dean casually took his place at the head of the table, pulled a cigar from his tweed jacket, lit it, and said, "Betty, pass out the agenda."

Betty, a young woman at the other end of the table, jumped up and distributed the one-page agenda. She was one of the few people in the room that I knew. When I was a Ph.D. student in the NYU economics department, Betty was Netzer's secretary. When he became dean of GPA, he took her with him and appointed her assistant dean, the chief administrative officer of the school.

"Let's hope we can get through all this without too much discussion. I have a lot of work today," Betty said cheerfully but with a stern undertone. Most of the men were filling their pipes, while the two women lit up cigarettes.

"Before we get down to business in our first meeting since last spring, Dick, tell us about your trip to Italy and France this summer," said Simon Goldstein on the dean's right. Simon was the professor who had distracted me with his endless banal phone conversations floating through his always open office door when I worked on the Ford Foundation grant as a graduate student. I noticed some rolling of eyes as well as some expectant grins. The dean smiled expansively, blew cigar smoke into the air, and began.

"If you think there are good restaurants here in New York, you don't know what's good. A bad meal is impossible in Paris, maybe possible in Rome at glitzy tourist traps. Pied de Cochon is a hole-in-the-wall in the Marais near where we stayed in Paris. My first visit there I had escargot, frisée salad with lardons, and apple sausage with scalloped potatoes. Then the crème brûlée for dessert. You can't *imagine* a better meal, not in New York, not anywhere except Paris. The owner-cook, a gregarious woman, recommended a bottle of red wine from Gascony that isn't sold in the U.S.—perfect. The four of us knocked down two bottles."

This was received with appreciative nods by some, as well as poker-faced silence by others. I was staring down at the so far blank pad I had brought with me for recording important issues.

"Oh, come on, Dick! You can afford a good Bordeaux—a Saint-Émilion or a Saint-Estèphe," said a jovial professor, removing the pipe from his mouth.

Sputtering angrily, the dean replied, "Bordeaux wine is overrated. Generations of interbreeding grape vines has produced foul tasting grape juice laced with alcohol."

"That's not what Orly Ashenfelter says in his wine newsletter," the jovial professor said. I knew Orly Ashenfelter as a prominent labor economist at Princeton who was also editor of the *American Economic Review*, the premier economic journal. I was to learn that he had also developed a model to predict wine prices.

"Orly Ashenfelter's ignorance of good wine is only exceeded by his ignorance of labor economics," snorted the dean. The appreciative crowd laughed, the others remained silent. I was stunned but silent. Ashenfelter was a neoclassical economist with impeccable credentials. Was Netzer critical of neoclassical economics? I was surprised.

When most teenagers were picking up social graces, Dean Netzer was picking up degrees. He graduated from the University of Wisconsin at seventeen, went on to Harvard earning a master's degree in urban planning and a Ph.D. in economics.

Originally appointed in the economics department of NYU in the 1960s, Netzer was made head of a search committee for a new dean of the Graduate School of Public Administration, partly because of his interest in public sector issues and his background in urban planning. Unsurprisingly, after a careful screening of candidates, Netzer found himself as best suited for the post, and the rest of the committee agreed. He became dean of that college in 1969.

"Tell us about Italy," urged Simon, the associate dean.

The professor sitting next to me whispered to the one on the other side, "Someone should kick Simon under the table, preferably in the balls, so he stops encouraging this food monologue."

"Simon doesn't have any balls. He's the dean's eunuch," replied the other professor. The scene now struck me as less intimidating than bizarre. Having never before attended a faculty meeting, I assumed the discussion would be about appointments, curriculum, and university policies. Instead it reminded me of elementary school discussions about what I did last summer. Would Netzer open the floor to other professors' accounts of their summer travels?

"Oh, in the Italian Riviera we had lunch at this four-star beach restaurant beyond elegance with exquisite pasta dishes and caprese. In walks a drunk German with his wife in tow. They sit down at a table, both in bathing suits, tee shirts, and no shoes. He bellows for a waiter. Before he can order drinks, the waiter apologizes and says they do not serve people in bathing suits. The German swears loudly at him. Then two more waiters come over and hustle the couple out the door!" said the dean, smiling happily.

From the other end of the table Betty announced, "OK. The first item on our agenda is revision of the core curriculum. You all got the Curriculum Committee's report with its recommendations in your mailboxes a few weeks ago. Of course, you have all read that and are prepared to vote today." I noted an edge in her voice.

"No! We first must vote to either *accept* the committee's report or to send it back to them for revision. Robert's Rules apply so long as I am member of this faculty, so help me God!" I was startled by the speaker's booming voice, coming as it did from the shortest man in the room. Bleached blond hair, flashy huge diamond ring, gold cuff links and matching tie pin all set him apart from the tweedy, but somewhat threadbare, male faculty around the table. He looked like Liberace might on a subdued day.

Betty looked exasperated. A frumpy bald man said with irritation, "Wait a minute Tony, we on the Curriculum Committee worked on that over the summer. We have nothing more to add. What is your problem with our report?"

"My problem? It tears the intellectual heart out of our master's program, making my Administrative Law course an elective instead of a core requirement, that's my problem!" Tony boomed. "When I was in law school and took administrative law, the scales fell from my eyes. My professor, Adrian Fifthnus, showed me that the central core, the guiding light, of wise governance is administrative law. Fifthnus and Pressner wrote the textbook I continue to use."

The jaundiced professor on my right whispered to me, "Shoutin' Shorty Tony was in law school in the Dark Ages, and never managed to graduate. He has been using that textbook for twenty years along with his yellow, brittle notes from law school."

The dean intervened. "Does anyone else have objections to the Curriculum Committee's fine report?"

Betty glowered threateningly. Murmurs of "no."

"Tony, why don't you write something up on your objections to the committee's report and submit it to us before the next meeting? We will put this agenda item over until then," said the dean.

Tony smiled and waved a sheaf of papers. "I *have* written something up—forty pages, single spaced. It is like a legal brief. Carefully reasoned, well documented, with ninety-two citations. I've worked days and nights on this since reading the committee's report, and I must say it is airtight. If Justice Frankfurter were still alive, I would send it to him as a model of legal reasoning. If my colleagues give this the attention it deserves, I feel confident they will be persuaded my position is the correct one. It will be in your mailboxes this afternoon."

"Send my copy to Justice Frankfurter, burdening his days in the hereafter," whispered the professor on my right.

Chapter Thirteen

The Dean and Some Others

After that first faculty meeting, I gradually became familiar with the dean and the faculty. You might think I was already very familiar with Dean Netzer as he had been my dissertation advisor, but I was not. In the two years I was writing my dissertation I probably had three or four meetings with him, and none lasted more than ten minutes.

The dean dressed as if he had bought all of his clothes at Brooks Brothers in 1959. Tweed jackets, gray flannel slacks, Oxford cloth shirts with button down collars, brown brogues that probably each weighed five pounds, and knit neckties in dark colors. On his casual days of no classes, the Oxford dress shirt and knit tie were replaced by a cashmere knit turtleneck, invariably beige.

Conversations with the dean could be difficult and awkward, until I caught on. People who graduate from college at seventeen are unlikely to be engaging and disarming in personal interactions. As I quickly learned, catching on meant hitting the dean with a question.

Not "How are you?' but a question such as, "Why doesn't New York State reform the property tax assessment process?" or "Do you think the incidence of the payroll tax varies with the tightness of the labor market?" Then the dean would take off and I would be free to daydream about something else, occasionally nodding and uttering "Uh-huh."

These conversations required no input from me—no bon mots, astute observations, or provocative objections—I could be asleep as long as that was not apparent. They were not really conversations but rather invitations to the dean to give a lecture, an invitation he never declined. Such lectures invariably included a withering denouncement of Congress or a mayor for their slothful ignorance. He was not paranoid. Stupid behavior was never attributed to ulterior, self-serving motives but to ignorance. He relished rooting out and exposing ignorance as well as stupidity.

I did not suspect him of stupidity just as I did not suspect him of prudent circumspection. Once at a faculty meeting he launched a tirade against a clerk he had recently encountered in a Hallmark card shop over some trivial matter. He asserted indignantly that all card shop clerks were similarly cognitively challenged. I thought that as an economist, it was puzzling that he expected something different. Those with the talent and education to be rocket scientists or even stockbrokers do not seek jobs in Hallmark card shops, except perhaps part-time while pursuing higher education. Speaking and reading English, the ability to make change, and the absence of a felony record are sufficient qualifications for long-term work there.

As I surmised at the first faculty meeting, the paunchy professor on the dean's right, Simon, who urged him to relate his European trip that summer, was the dean's sycophant—in fact his favorite sycophant, I learned from other faculty. He was a bright, lazy, gossip with only a bachelor's degree in economics from some college in western Canada. Somehow the dean got him appointed as an assistant professor. Producing nothing in the years leading up to tenure, the dean arranged for him to edit a book of light-weight articles on urban economics. He was tenured and promoted to full professor. The dean overstepped some years later when he awarded that fellow with appointment as head of the Ph.D. program. When the Ph.D. students learned that Simon with meager academic output and only a bachelor's degree, was the director of doctoral studies, they were furious. A delegation of Ph.D. students appeared at a smoke-filled faculty meeting and argued, with dignity but animation, that it was insulting and unfair to have as director someone with far less formal education than themselves. The dean was uncharacteristically quiet. Shortly thereafter, the dean removed his sycophant from that post and replaced him with a professor who did have a Ph.D., a drinking problem, and a similarly meager record of publication.

But the favorite sycophant, Simon, was awarded with a new post—associate dean of the school. With that job there came a grand office with an eighteen-foot ceiling, a marble fireplace, an oriental rug, and two grand windows overlooking Washington Square Park. So ensconced, Simon spent the next eight years chatting with students, faculty, and visitors, and losing important papers. The dean, with his many outside interests and an impressive publication record, probably spent one day a week running the school, delegating all else to the associate dean.

Another of the dean's sycophants, Betty, who began as his secretary in the Economics Department and was brought along to the Graduate School of Public Administration when Netzer became the dean, was promoted by him to be the assistant dean, a non-faculty position that amounts to the chief administrative officer of the school. As she explained to me (we had become friendly when I was still a graduate student in the economic department and she was a secretary there), she quickly realized that Simon the associate dean was dysfunctional. Rather than confront the dean with the consequences of his bad choice, she arranged with a secretary of the associate dean to have no papers of any consequence, requiring competent and speedy action, to ever *ever* be delivered to him. They all went to her.

She was efficient, competent, and slavishly loyal to the dean. With the dean engaged elsewhere and the associate dean permanently disengaged, Betty ran the college.

In the third year after his deanship appointment, Netzer won a large, three-year, National Science Foundation grant to analyze and forecast energy demand in the greater New York region. That was the time of the first energy crisis beginning in 1973, when world oil prices were quadrupled. Various faculty in the college were included on that grant, and the dean was the principal investigator. Senior professors appointed to that research project did little. Junior faculty and their Ph.D. students did most of the work. The dean presided over occasional meetings that he would call about the project. In the week before the final report was due, he wrote a breezy fifteen-page summary of the findings.

I was one of the junior faculty selected by the dean to do two of the sub-parts of the project. In those three years, I had a single one-on-one conversation with him about the project, which lasted five minutes. I expressed my frustration to Simon about receiving so little direction from the dean about the project, and he said to me, "That is the dean's style. He works alone. A large, collaborative grant under him is destined to fail."

I became close friends with Manny Tobier, somewhat senior to me on the faculty, who had also been a graduate student in economics at NYU before my time there. He was smart, energetic, and a crack researcher. Manny had impressed the dean when both were in the economics department. They shared a professional fascination with the evolving economic and demographic profile of New York City. The dean had been Manny's dissertation advisor on a study of the housing market in the city including the effects of rent control. In the same period, the dean was working on a book about the economic effects of the property tax nationwide. Manny was his key research assistant on that empirical analysis. The book was published by the prestigious Brookings Institute, and received much favorable attention among public finance economists. As a result, the dean became a highly recognized scholar among economists.

After finishing graduate school, Manny was appointed as an

assistant professor at Queens College. He also became an economic consultant with the Regional Plan Association (RPA), a nonprofit that analyzed the New York regional economy. The dean was on the RPA board. In one of my ten-minute meetings with the dean during work on my dissertation, some data issue came up that Netzer thought I should talk to Manny about. I visited Manny at his RPA office, meeting him for the first time. Entering his office, a chaotic mess of papers and books, it seemed to be unoccupied, and so I called out "Manny?" A bald head emerged from behind a stack of computer printouts.

"I am hiding from co-workers who want to chat about baseball. You must be Matt."

"Yes, and I am not here to chat about baseball. I need some data that Netzer thinks you can get for me."

"Probably so. I have data up to my eyeballs," he said.

Manny proved to be a goldmine for data I could use. We spent an hour discussing my research. I liked him immediately.

Manny's dissertation interested me. To most mainstream economists, rent control was anathema because it distorted the market for housing. As a social liberal, that was OK with me. The problem was the unintended consequences of hurting the poor and helping the well-off.

After I was on the faculty, one of my lectures in my required microeconomics course was about those unintended ill effects of residential rent control on low-income households. Rental housing in low income neighborhoods turns over rapidly because the poor move a lot. Controlled rents could be increased each time a unit became vacant. So in such rapid turnover neighborhoods, the rent level was probably similar to what it would be in a free market. In stable neighborhoods with low turnover, rent control levels were far under market rents bestowing a windfall on renters. I would relate egregious anecdotes to my class about well-off New York renters who could afford second homes in the country thanks to rent control.

Manny had a Ph.D. in economics of course but he was positively hostile to the profession of academic economists. In the 1970s the economics department at NYU hired elderly stars away from more prestigious universities, such as Wassily Leontief from Harvard and William Baumol from Princeton. Manny dubbed it "the valley of the bones." He sometimes was assigned to teach the required economics course that I taught as well. While I always assigned an economics textbook that was not too difficult for GPA students, Manny assigned *The Wall Street Journal* as the main reading for his section. He explained to me that "They'll learn more about real world economics that way." Scornful as he was of academic neoclassical economics, he was a gifted natural economist. That is, he perceived fundamental economic issues under the blur of public policy discussions.

When New York City reformed its strict rent control regulations, Manny saw the bad economic effects of the old rent control on the supply of rental housing and on turnover of tenants. Old apartment buildings dating from before World War II, which accounted for more than half of the housing stock in the city, were subject to rent control. All new buildings were free from rent control. As a result, perfectly solid apartment buildings were torn down by owners and replaced with new buildings to escape rent control. Manny endorsed the new rent stabilization program, a form of reasonable rent control that allowed modest increases in residential rents. The city appointed him to chair the Rent Stabilization Board, responsible for setting the annual increases based on a number of factors.

It turned out to be a thankless task. Landlords always complained that the allowed rent increases were too low, and organized renters always complained that they were too high. Manny began to receive angry phone calls at home. He stopped having his telephone number listed, and eventually he resigned from the Rent Stabilization Board. Of course, rent control of any kind is anathema to neoclassical economists, as is a minimum wage. Both are interferences in the efficient operation of free markets. But in my discussions with Manny, I came to see that the free markets hypothesized in neoclassical economics do not exist outside of agriculture. That realization did not occur to me as a Ph.D. student in economics, but it gradually did at GPA. As I focused on public policy issues, I realized that the market could *not* solve all public policy problems.

Taking my cue from Netzer, I did a good deal of outside consulting while on the faculty of GPA. Because the earliest classes were at 4:20 p.m., and classes met only once a week for two hours, it was easy to fit in full days of outside consulting. Most of mine were with my former employer, W. R. Grace, in their economics department.

The person David Elkin hired to replace me in 1971, Duncan

Bailey, was a recent Ph.D. economics graduate from George Mason University. Duncan was an outspoken conservative whom I came to like, despite his extreme political views. I suspect much of what he said was aimed at agitating me, knowing that I was a liberal. What impressed me most at first was the fact that as a graduate student he was the co-author of an article published in the leading journal, *American Economic Review*. The other author was an economics professor at George Mason. I became less impressed as I realized that professors often used graduate students as slaves at the oars to do the research required to help turn out articles.

Duncan despised the public sector. He thought that public school teachers' pay scale should be similar to babysitters. While in graduate school, he made money by organizing a placement agency for housekeepers. He bragged about ripping off his mostly immigrant clients. Duncan was the most politically incorrect person I knew, and he wore it as a badge of honor. I was amused by his outrageous remarks about teachers (dumb), taxes (always too high), and government workers (slothful and venal). *He can't be serious,* I thought at first. *He simply says those things to provoke me.*

In the first Reagan administration, 1981–84, Peter Grace paid for a full-page ad in *The New York Times* supporting Reagan's massive income tax cut. Like Reagan, Peter apparently believed that government was the problem to be attacked. In 1982, Reagan established a commission to rein in federal spending. He named Peter Grace as its head, so it came to be known as the Grace Commission. The commission's final report was released in January, 1984. It made many recommendations to curtail or streamline federal government programs. The savings in federal government outlays were estimated at a whopping $424 billion over three years. Most of those so-called savings were by cutting social welfare programs such as food stamps. Most of Grace's proposals were rejected by Congress, I was happy to learn.

Peter Grace was not a liberal. He had attacked the food stamp program as a giveaway to Puerto Ricans. Peter had chosen Duncan, thanks to his outspoken conservative opinions, to identify wasteful federal spending. Ironically, Peter made sure that the hours of work that Duncan and others in the Grace economics and finance divisions did for his study was paid for by W. R. Grace. So, stockholders, not taxpayers, paid for the Grace report. It reminded me of all the fact checking we GM employees did on the stockholders' dime for Alfred Sloan's book, *My Years with General Motors*.

Chapter Fourteen

The Dean's Clash with Manny

In addition to loudly arguing points before the assembled faculty as if they were a rapt jury, Tony fancied himself a skillful negotiator. An angry impasse between the dean and a group of senior professors, led by their most sensible, and tallest, member—Manny—provided Tony his great opportunity to negotiate a settlement.

Some years before, the dean had hired a young woman for an entry-level faculty position. (All entry level positions were filled by the dean.) No review or vote by the faculty was required. It may have been required by the university, but no one objected, but they did grouse among themselves. She turned out to be another Netzer sycophant, and so of course he was fond of her. When she came up for tenure in 1974 with a few unimpressive publications, the personnel committee, chaired by Manny, voted her down. The dean was livid. Rather than confront the personnel committee and its leader, he shot off an angry, vituperative memo to Manny, who shared it with me and the committee. He replied firmly, but not in kind, refusing to reconsider the matter. The dean sent an even more intemperate memo, to which Manny did not reply. But Manny did not actually ignore the dean's memo. Rather it festered like a poisoned, rusty knife in his skull for the rest of his long career.

After their clash on the tenure issue, they hated each other with an unspoken passion. Unspoken to each other that is. Manny spoke his hatred to anyone who would listen. The dean was uncharacteristically circumspect. The one negative remark I ever heard from the dean about Manny was this: "I got him every job he ever had. No good deed goes unpunished." The irony here was that they were both very good empirical economists and both quite skeptical about neoclassical theory, and so they should have been intellectual allies. They both contributed to my growing disenchantment with neoclassical economics.

Tony savored his self-appointed role to negotiate an accommodation between the personnel committee, of which he was a member, and the dean. Despite the hours, days and months Tony spent at that effort, it came to naught. Neither the dean nor the committee would agree to a compromise. That was OK with Tony because it was the process that he loved, not the outcome.

Manny attempted to win my membership in his club of faculty who despised the dean. In that effort he related other incidents of the dean's highhanded behavior. I declined to sign on. My last word on the issue was, "He's the only dean I have ever had, and so I can't compare his behavior with anyone else's."

I realize now that was a dumb answer, but an answer characteristic of an economist who taught statistics. Nothing could be inferred from one observation. But something else was at work: loyalty to Netzer.

Above: My first home on West Grand Boulevard in Detroit, 1939.

Left: Me at summer cottage in Belle River, Ontario, 1940.

Me addressing a seminar of mine at Cornell University Department of Urban Planning, circa 1996.

My summer house in Wellfleet, Massachusetts. Spent every summer there since 1995.

My daughter Maureen, my daughter Erica, probably three years old, my son Matthew in our Ithaca NY home, 1992.

Left to right, my son Matthew, my wife Katherine Stone, Erica Drennan our daughter, Maureen Drennan my daughter.

Me and my wife, Katherine, on our deck in Wellfleet, August 2020.

Chapter Fifteen

The Fall of the Dean

Another junior faculty member, Brenda, was considerably older than the others, having come to academia late in life. She was an aggressive, outspoken liberal who made other liberals become conservative. What Randall Jarrell wrote about the novelist Mary McCarthy, faintly disguised as a fictional character at a college, captured Brenda perfectly. "It was not that her bark was worse than her bite. Her bark was her bite."

Brenda was unlucky in love, and her former husband more so. President of a small Catholic college, independently wealthy, he had a long affair with a nun, which says something about Brenda's qualities as a wife. When Brenda discovered his affair, she booted him out, and in the divorce she won the house, the kids, and the tennis court. For those who knew Brenda, he was the clear winner. The children were not. Faculty who inadvertently overheard Brenda's conversations with her eldest son on the phone had their ears scorched. Unsympathetic, unsupportive, and forever shrill, she was not the mother Hallmark had in mind in producing their saccharine Mother's Day cards.

The new president of the university, John Sawhill, a hard-charging conservative, was an energy expert. He was eager to become involved in the dean's National Science Foundation (NSF) energy research grant, and the dean was happy to have him participate. Brenda was one of the junior faculty involved in the project. When she learned that the president wanted to participate, she thrust herself forward to be his collaborator. Naturally, the president came to hate her, not because she didn't produce, but rather the torrent of drafts that she sent him on various aspects of the research issue that all concluded with a denouncement of American capitalism, which in the 1970s was a timid, toothless affair compared with today's virulent variety. The president probably felt that the dean was responsible for that collaboration made in hell, and held that against him. What the president did not realize was that the dean was far from a hands-on manager of his research team. The dean did not sic Brenda upon the president. She was unassisted in her attack.

The president was to get more grief for which he blamed the dean, this time rightly so. Speaking truth to power is one of the best things academics can do, and the dean did it. He was asked by the governor of New York, Hugh Carey, to do a major analysis of the property tax system in the state, which the state financed. The governor had pushed through the legislature a major reform of that tax five years earlier. He was eager to get vindication for his reforms through an independent, expert evaluation. The dean produced a cogent, well-supported study establishing that the property tax reforms were a disaster, depressing property values and reducing construction in the state. The governor never released the report, and I heard that he complained loudly to Sawhill, the NYU President, about the dean. Being a modern university president, Sawhill did not defend the dean to the governor, so I was told. Backbone is not a prerequisite for the position of university president.

The final event that drove the president to get rid of the dean was a public forum that Sawhill organized on municipal transit systems, focusing particularly on the New York City subway system which was barely functioning and hemorrhaging money at that time. Sawhill selected one of his favorite NYU economics professors to deliver a paper he had written promoting privatization of the subway system. The audience of one hundred distinguished guests in the law school conference hall included New York City notables such as the former mayor John Lindsay. Netzer, the dean, was on the panel selected to comment on the paper. The professor's presentation was an unsurprising denigration of bad management and under investment by the city government for the sorry state of the subway system. His solution was to sell the subway system to a private sector firm, arguing that privatizing the system would make it more efficient, would provide better service, and generate profits.

This view was an expression of public choice theory, all the rage back then among neoclassical economists. That school of thought presumed that government officials acted in their own self-interest, denying any sort of public interest motive. Therefore, government was not to be trusted to improve economic outcomes.

When I was a graduate student enamored of neoclassical economics, public choice theory was not yet popular among economists. But since my graduate student days, the increasing conservatism among the profession made public choice theory attractive because it favored market solutions rather than government solutions to economic problems. Hence the increased support among economists for privatization and deregulation. I did not join that camp. Nor did I denigrate people who honestly and altruistically pursued the public interest in their careers. That characterization would apply to most of our Ph.D. students at GPA, now the Wagner School of NYU. As an economist in a school focused upon the public sector, I did not embrace public choice theory.

In his comments, Netzer's opening was one of his withering zingers. "This paper is an example of why economics has won such a bad name. There is not the thinnest tissue of fact over this theoretical romp." He then went on to give a history of the subway system—how it was built with substantial public subsidy; how it was originally privately held by a few firms that watered their stock and then went bankrupt; how New York City reluctantly took over the system rather than face the transportation nightmare of having it cease operation. That story is an example of why graduate students in economics should learn some economic history.

Tone deaf to attacks based on mere facts, the economics professor was not chagrinned or angry. But President Sawhill was angry. As a zealous free market economist himself, he was determined to spread the gospel of smaller government and privatization in American cities, especially in the bastion of liberalism: New York City. Sawhill had picked the dean to comment on it because of Netzer's status as an eminent public finance economist. The president assumed that Netzer would endorse privatization of the subway system, which he did not do. The dean was not a free market ideologue (and neither was I by then, 1980), and he always spoke his mind, never gently.

Netzer was well into his third five-year term when Sawhill decided to get rid of him. The formal review process he organized was more elaborate than most. A committee of three outside professors, selected by the president, were to interview every GPA faculty member privately about the dean. The knives came out. Actually, not knives but copies of intemperate memos that the dean had shot off to various faculty members upbraiding them for one offense or another, some serious, some trivial. These were eagerly provided to the outside committee. Manny, who had been nursing his hatred of the dean for years, a hatred spawned by a tenure case in which Manny, as head of the personnel committee, had turned down a candidate Netzer favored. In response, Netzer sent Manny a series of scalding memos—and the outside committee's report used these to bolster the president's decision to remove him.

Netzer's deanship ended in 1982. As a tenured faculty member, he continued to be a presence, though removed from power. He was appointed head of the new (1982) Center for Urban Studies at GPA, funded by a one million-dollar, five-year grant from the Revson Foundation. The faculty found him more agreeable in his defanged condition. He maintained a low profile with the new dean, aloof and reserved.

Chapter Sixteen

Moving from the Forest to Greenwich Village and Block Island

At the end of my first academic year at GPA, we moved from our rented house in the forest primeval of Putnam County to NYU housing in Greenwich Village. For me, it was a blessed change. No more two-hour commutes. Instead my commute was almost more vertical than horizontal. We lived on the 10th floor of one of the three NYU Silver Towers buildings at 110 Bleecker Street. My office was on the seventh floor of the new Tisch Hall, one block away. For my wife and my son it was a cursed change. To now see only flocks of starlings and pigeons each day in our new home on Bleecker Street was for them depressing.

My wife realized that for me it was better to end the grueling commute, but not without extracting my promise that every summer we would somehow take our two children out of the city—not for a flimsy two-week vacation but for the entire summer. How I could afford to do that was a mystery, but I reluctantly promised to do it. Part of the reason I agreed was that she told me that her doctor announced to her that she had a heart condition that would kill her in five to ten years. I was determined to make her happy before her death. I believed her. It was not true.

By the time we moved into Silver Towers, our daughter Maureen was walking. Really she was running; she hardly ever walked. I didn't approve of putting kids who could walk in strollers. It seemed so indolent. So I would often take Maureen for walks, but immediately a problem arose. When Matt Jr. started walking with me, there was never a dispute over what direction we should take. I was the decider. But Maureen would invariably choose to take off in the opposite direction from me. Of course she would be running, so I had to run after her, catch her, and plant her in the right direction and get her out of harm's way. That happened more than once, so I found our walks exhausting. But that was still preferable to pushing her in a stroller like some little Nero.

At dinner we often talked about world affairs. Maureen could talk, but she had little to contribute on such topics. One evening we were discussing how East Pakistan had seceded from Pakistan and became Bangladesh. Maureen looked incredulous and said: "bang-a-dish!"

As I had done with Matt Jr., I sometimes read Bible stories to Maureen at bedtime. Moses getting the Ten Commandments was one. "What's the Ten Commandments?" she asked me. I explained that they were rules God wanted us to obey. "Oh, I know one of them!" she said excitedly.

"What is that?" I was curious.

"And don't suck your thumb!"

When Maureen was five and her brother Matt Jr. was fifteen, she had a friend in the building named Maya. Maya had an older brother, Ravi, who was a bully. One day when he and Maya were playing with Maureen in our apartment, he pocketed one of Maureen's treasured Star Wars figures. When Maureen later discovered it was missing and rightly believed that Maya's brother was the culprit, she implored Matt Jr. to go to Maya's apartment and demand its return. Matt Jr. refused, telling Maureen to steel up her courage and go herself. She agreed if Matt Jr. would go with her. Here is the account Matt Jr. later gave me of the confrontation later that day.

He told Maureen, "I will stand where they can't see me in the hallway, and *you* ask him to return your toy."

"Okay, I will," said Maureen. She rang the doorbell of Maya's apartment while Matt Jr. was not visible but within earshot. The brother, Ravi, answered the door.

"Hi Maureen."

"Ravi, my big brother said you've got to give me back my Star Wars toy, and he is right down this hall waiting!" Ravi complied with no objection.

Maureen clearly understood about power. I was beginning to learn about it. In the neoclassical economics model there is no power outside of the impersonal free market that determines all prices based on supply and demand. Neither producers nor consumers can influence those outcomes. But I realized, contrary to what I learned in graduate school, that corporations, especially large ones, have enormous market power. In the past, that was partly offset by labor union power, but no longer.

Although I was beginning to learn about power, tools and machinery were mostly foreign to me and I had no intention to correct that ignorance. When my son was a teenager he was mortified in car repair shops by my obvious and freely expressed ignorance of the mechanical workings of cars. He sensed the mechanic's quiet contempt of me. Perhaps that is why he learned to do so many things that I cannot do: sail a boat, work on a fishing boat, build a house.

As I had promised my supposedly dying wife after moving from Putnam Valley to NYU housing in Greenwich Village, we rented a house on Block Island for the entire summer of 1973 and many summers thereafter. We did not own a car once we moved back to Manhattan, and I was dead set against owning a car because of the expense. So, we needed to find a summer place accessible without a car, and where we could get around on bikes. Fire Island and Block Island were obvious choices. We rejected Fire Island because on trips there to visit friends, we found it to be mostly lacking in grocery stores and without a movie theater. We had been to Block Island one summer weekend and we loved it. The Amtrak New York to Boston train stopped in New London where we could take a two-hour ferry to Block Island. The train also stopped in Westerly, Rhode Island, where we could take a cab to the airport for the ten-minute flight to Block Island. The planes were small, one or two engines, carrying three to eight passengers.

That first summer we rented a simple modern cottage with a huge yard right on the ocean. It was biking distance from town and close to the town beach, where there was a lifeguard, a changing room, and a snack bar. The ocean was warm there because of the Gulf Stream. But Maureen, almost two that summer, was not happy at the beach. She would invariably take a handful of sand, put it in her mouth, spit it out, cry and repeat. We got her a small inflatable pool for the yard, and left her home with the babysitter, Gwyn Wilson, while the rest of us went to the beach.

I had never, in my thirty-six years, eaten a mussel but I came to love them that summer. We collected them off rocks in knee-deep water at low tide, scrubbed off the sand and hair, and steamed them in garlic and olive oil. We ate a lot of mussels and blue fish, the cheapest fish at the fish market. They are very oily, but when they are doused with milk and baked, they taste grand.

As I noted, in Putnam Valley my wife, Brigid, and son, Matt Jr., had become enthusiastic and skilled birders; myself less so. Block Island was the perfect place for birding, especially in the migration of late summer and autumn. Late summer, shore birds from the far north Atlantic coast passed through Block Island in thousands—Sandpipers, Greater and Lesser Yellowlegs, Herons, Plovers and others. In autumn thousands of Warblers descended, some to their premature death. Migration is fatal for many small birds. In the autumn I have seen one or two Peregrine Falcons patiently waiting on the south bluffs of Block Island for exhausted warblers to tumble out of the sky, exhausted because, migrating at night, they missed the point where the New England coast turns west. With the rising sun, they see they are over the ocean, and so they turn back. The first land they see is Block Island. And the Falcons await their arrival.

At the end of the summer of 1973, we learned that the cottage we rented would not be available the following summer, so we had to find another. On the train ride back to New York around Labor Day, Brigid sat with Mrs. Connolly with whom she had been chatting on the platform before the train arrived. Mrs. Connolly and her husband owned two houses on Block Island. We passed them each day riding to town or the beach. The one they occupied in the summer was big, but nothing special. The other one, next door, was a beautiful Victorian with a swing for two on the front porch. We loved it. That was the one they had been renting out. By the end of the train trip, Mrs. Connolly agreed to rent it to us every summer. Brigid could be quite charming when she put her mind to it. So we rented the Connolly house for the next five years.

The house had splendid ocean views, old-fashioned stuffed furniture, a serviceable kitchen, and a grand bathroom on the second floor with bead board walls and a large claw-foot bathtub. The bedroom we assigned to Maureen had an enormous desk, a gift from Mussolini to Joe Connolly's dad, a former Hearst newspaper editor who interviewed Il Duce in the 1930s. Given that the interview was by a Hearst paper, it was doubtless favorable if not glowing. Joe Connolly was a gregarious recovering alcoholic and an unsuccessful entrepreneur who talked endlessly and optimistically about his current deals. Mrs. Connolly was subdued and oblivious of other people, such as her tenants. She was the head of the New York City's Bronx Botanical Garden, and quite knowledgeable about flowers and plants. Joe had a set of drums out in his garage that he sometimes played, never softly. He bragged that he had been the drummer in Artie Shaw's band in the 1940s.

One summer they invited us to one of their large parties. Suddenly Brigid grabbed my arm and whispered, "Mrs. Connolly is taking a couple into our house! Stop her!" Dutifully I went across the yard to our house. The intruders were already on the second floor. It was somewhat messy as to be expected on a weekend in a summer house.

"Oh, sorry for the mess. Brigid will be mortified," I said. They took the hint and left. Brigid was enraged after we left the party, blaming me for Mrs. Connolly's tactless intrusion. I had become accustomed to receiving blame for much that was wrong in the world. Arguing was ineffectual. I departed for a bar until she calmed down.

The year-round population of Block Island was about seven hundred. At the northern tip of the island there was a stone monument listing the names of the original settler families in 1661. Some of the current residents had those names and were mighty proud of it too. One woman I knew there who came to Block Island as an adult told me she had never been accepted as an islander. When she complained to an islander about that snubbing, carried forward to her children who were born on Block Island, he said, "Well if yer cat birthed kittens in the oven, would ya call 'em biscuits?"

Every summer I taught the maximum of two courses, statistics and economics, in summer school in order to afford the Block Island rental. Summer school was eight weeks in June and July. On weekends I would go to Block Island, and then for the whole month of August.

Chapter Seventeen

The New York City Economy, 1975–1988

In the spring of 1975, my NYU colleague Manny and I met with a New York City Office of Management and Budget (OMB) senior official. The purpose was to provide her with our final report on our study of housing in New York that OMB had funded. Manny was the principal investigator while I was his assistant. The three of us met in a conference room of the Municipal Building. While talking about our report, the door opened and an ashen-faced young woman addressed the senior official: "The banks won't accept our notes!"

That was the beginning of the famous New York City fiscal crisis. Contrary to past practice, the large New York banks refused to fund further borrowing by the city, borrowing that had grown year after year. The main reason for the excessive borrowing was that the city's economy had falling employment starting in 1970 that continued every year through 1977—eight years of a shrinking economy. It was not a recession, a short-lived downturn, it was a depression.

From 3.8 million jobs in 1969, city employment fell to 3.2 million in 1977. Population tumbled as well. In the 1970 census the city had 7.9 million people. By 1980 it was down to 7.1 million, a drop of 0.8 million. Crime was on the rise. There was an epidemic of burning tenement housing in the Bronx, some due to arson by landlords. Many stores along 5th Avenue below 42nd Street were vacant. Subway ridership declined, partly due to crime in the subway. Another negative development was the flood of corporate headquarters departing for other cities and suburbs. In 1965, New York City was home to 129 of the Fortune 500 headquarters. By 1975, the count was down to 62. That trend alarmed city leaders, both public and private.

In 1975, I had been hired by the Conservation of Human Resources (CHR), at Columbia University as a senior researcher. Like me, the entire senior staff was professors. The CHR was headed by Eli Ginzberg, a professor at the Columbia Business School and a noted expert on labor issues. Ginzberg negotiated a grant from the Rockefeller Brothers Fund (RBF) to do a study of the flight of corporate headquarters from New York. The study would include interviews with top executives of headquarters that had departed as well as headquarters still located in New York. The RBF was not a passive funder. The woman assigned to oversee the study, Marilyn Levy, took a major role in directing our work. She and Ginzberg put together a panel of prominent corporate executives, including commercial real estate leaders in the city. The panel met with us every month or so to hear of our progress and make suggestions. Most important, they put together the list of corporations to be interviewed and won their permission for us to interview a senior executive. I was assigned to do all of the interviews. I was also the major author of the final report, carefully edited by Chuck Brecher, a New School political science professor and CHR staff researcher. I was so impressed with him that a few years later I urged Netzer, the dean of GPA, to add him to our faculty, which he did in 1980.

The final report, *The Corporate Headquarters Complex in New York City*, was published in 1977. It was not a gloomy story as I had thought it would be. We called it "complex" because in doing the interviews, I learned that headquarters that departed New York continued to employ the services of New York firms: in finance, law, advertising, consulting, accounting, publishing, and headhunting. They changed to local providers for routine services such as payrolls. So the technology that made corporate headquarters more footloose, such as jet travel, made the high-level service firms in New York more competitive nationally and even internationally. There was a time when California advertising agencies dominated the west coast market. No longer. They have been taken over or pushed out by New York advertising agencies. This revelation informed the rest of my academic career. That is, high-level services, now called producer services, have become central to most of my urban economic publications of the past four decades.

Two of the CHR staff, Chuck Brecher and Ray Horton of the Columbia Business School, launched an annual volume, *Setting Municipal Priorities (SMP),* in 1979. It was an edited collection of papers they sponsored about New York City. Most of the authors were professors. The first chapter of each annual edition was on the city's economy, written by me. Chuck and Ray, both political scientists, were the editors and often wrote pieces for the volume. The book came out in November or December each year and was accompanied by a weekend gala conference at the august Harriman House, a short drive north of New York City. Local and state politicians, appointed city officials, notables, reporters, and authors were in attendance. *The New York Times* always ran a story with photos from the conference. Other city newspapers often ran a story about the book or conference. During the Koch administration, a *Daily News* article about one of the pieces in the book had this headline: "Prof Says Koch Balances Budget on Backs of Poor." That was the last SMP conference attended by Mayor Koch, and he forbade anyone on his staff from attending.

In a city and state where politics is always contentious, Koch's boycott induced other politicians to attend. A regular attendee was the woman staff writer of *The New Yorker*, Andy Logan. She wrote the series "Around City Hall," covering the happenings in local government. At one SMP conference I was having a conversation with her and some others about Dorothy Parker. I regaled them with the Dorothy Parker story I had heard about her running into the editor and *The New Yorker* founder, Harold Ross, on the street in the early days of the magazine. "I thought you promised to come in one day and write us something," he said reproachfully.

"I was there! Someone was using the pencil."

My small audience laughed, except Andy Logan.

"That's not how I heard it," she said. "Her actual reply was, 'I was too fucking busy, and vice versa.'"

My annual forecast report and chapters in *SMP,* especially the latter, rendered me the go-to person on the city's economy in the 1980s. I was invited by the city's Office of Management and Budget (OMB) to be on their board of outside advisors on the city's economy. Most of the other members were low-level bank economists. But at one of our meetings, OMB had invited a distinguished Columbia University economist, William Vickrey. Some years later he was awarded the Nobel Memorial Award in economics. But at our meeting he was a dud. I think the topic was possible new revenue sources for the city government. Vickrey's contribution was to impose tolls on all bridges into the city, varying by time of day, and impose access fees on all vehicles south of 96th Street, also varying by time of day. His plan was a beautiful application of "marginal cost pricing" (his later Nobel award noted particularly his work on this topic). But it was dead on arrival for the city's OMB. Only the state government had the power to launch such a policy, and suburban legislators would never approve it. Someday it might happen, but not then. Experts on neoclassical economic theory I realized, were not suited for addressing public policy.

In the autumn of 1987 there was a sharp stock market drop, and my econometric model, fortified now by non-quantitative information about the city, was then pointing to an economic decline in 1988. I wanted to get the news out, I explained to my wife Kathy (yes, I had divorced and remarried, as I will explain soon). Maybe I should phone reporters and explain about my forecast report. Kathy, a former newspaper person before law school, shook her head and said, "Tell them you've changed your forecast."

"But they will say what forecast?" I objected.

"Never mind. Just say you've changed it."

It worked. I had almost two weeks of fame, starting with a short article in the *Daily News* followed by some other newspaper articles, an interview on a local TV news, and then an article in *The New York Times*. After that appeared, I got a call from CBS News. They sent a chauffeured car to pick me up and take me to the CBS studio. I was briefly interviewed on screen for the national evening news broadcast. The topic, of course, was the likely effect of the stock market crash on the New York City economy. The nation doesn't pay much attention to New York, so my appearance on CBS news was the beginning and end of my national fame.

But my local fame continued. As noted above, *The New York Times* subscribed to my annual forecast report on the city and regional economy. I was invited to make a presentation to the business side executives of the *Times* on the economic outlook for the city. The newspaper's executives were already worried about the local economy because their ad revenue was declining, I was told by some of them. Their premonition that the economy was softening was reinforced by my forecast report, and that is probably why they invited me to speak. Before I spoke, Mr. Sulzberger the publisher, introduced himself to me, said he might have to run out early, and thanked me for coming.

He stayed for the whole event including questions at the end.

To me, the fact that no one in that audience expressed a contrary view, i.e. the city's economy will be fine, reassured me in my forecast of an employment drop in 1988. But I was wrong. It turned out that there was an anemic rise of city employment in 1988—less than 1 percent. As Yogi Berra had supposedly said, "Forecasting is very risky—especially about the future."

Chapter Eighteen

The Divorce

"I SIGNED THE divorce papers today and mailed them to my attorney," Brigid said calmly. It was August 1981. I was stunned. She had been threatening divorce whenever she lost her temper with me, which was often, for the past twenty years. To say it calmly was stunning.

I knew it must be true. Divorce threats, like suicide threats, dissipated so long as there were some remaining acts left for her to perform, not me. I found her the attorney after much badgering. I laid out for him the divorce plans. I never believed it would happen after so many years of crying wolf. So there was one last act for her to perform: sign the divorce papers and mail them back. I believed she would never do it. I had performed my role of doing all the advance work so I could not be faulted. The last step was up to her. I knew she would never do it. Then she did it. We were divorced.

But I had a reprieve that I thought optimistically might be permanent. My wife asked me to stay on in our NYU apartment until she finished writing her book about birding and to help out with our daughter Maureen, who was then ten years old. Brigid had been writing the book for two years. I thought she might never finish it, and so we would continue living together forever despite our divorce. Another straw I was grasping was that I suspected she had not told her sisters or our friends about the divorce, a hint that she didn't really want me out of her life. If I had been sensible and realistic, I would have answered her request that I stay by saying, "No. I did not want this divorce, you did. So I'm leaving."

Was it love that kept me from accepting the divorce? No, I think it was grim, dark duty of my Catholic upbringing. At our wedding in a Catholic church, I had vowed to be with her "in sickness and in health till death do us part." Years before I had come to the realization that my wife was mentally unstable, perhaps bipolar. I stayed to protect her from herself, and protect the children from her, or so I told myself back then. The thought of taking her to a psychiatrist was anathema to my Catholic background, and hers too. "Taking" is the right word, because she would never willfully seek psychological attention.

Two months after the divorce, she calmly announced in October, "I want you to move out this week." I had no idea where I would go, but there was no disputing the deadline with her. Her book was published.

We had a friend, Sam Schoenbaum, a gay artist from Australia, who lined up all but two of the eleven short-term apartments I occupied in the first year following my displacement from the NYU apartment. We met Sam through a colleague of mine at NYU. My wife was desperate to find a competent draftsman to produce the many maps required for her book. The first one she used was an engineer, a draftsman. His maps were masterpieces of minimalism, not what one requires in a map whose purpose is to get you from A to B by car, foot, boat or all three. My colleague thought Sam would be up for that job, and indeed he was. Like most artists, Sam did not have a nine-to-five job. His was a gig economy before the phrase was created. We both liked Sam immediately, and she set him to work on producing the maps.

Sam had a wide network of friends in Greenwich Village and more affordable areas of the city. Most of them had apartments near NYU, and they traveled away from the city for parts of each year. They were happy to rent their digs for short stretches, sans any landlord approval, to anyone Sam vetted.

One day when I was walking with Sam to view my first short-term rental, he said, "You know Matt, now that you're divorced you need a girlfriend." I was stunned. The thought had never entered my mind. Probably because I continued to have the vain hope that the divorce was not permanent. Life after divorce was unimaginable to me. Winning my wife back would be compromised if I took a girlfriend. I feared that Sam would find me a girlfriend as easily as he found me apartments. So I did not ask for his matchmaker assistance.

The first apartment Sam got for me was a small walkup on 8th Avenue near 18th Street. I stayed there two weeks. I had never been in the apartment of a gay man before. When I saw the huge mirror over the double bed, I blushed. The permanent resident, whose name

I've forgotten, had a collection of gay comic books. The usual theme of his literature was serendipitous and mutual seduction between the main character and strangers: UPS delivery men, plumbers, etc. I was disappointed. I had thought gay men were more like Cole Porter or Noel Coward, discriminating in their choice of partners. The comic books were low and vulgar. I was not homophobic, but I was snobbish.

I grasped at another straw in December when my wife invited me to accompany her and our two kids to spend Christmas at our Block Island house (we had stopped renting and bought the house in 1978). We would all participate in the annual Christmas Bird Count on Block Island, a national event beloved of birders sponsored by the National Audubon Society. Some of our friends joined us on the island for the count, a one-day event scheduled between Christmas and New Year. We had everyone for dinner at the end of the count when the groups of two to four birders presented their tally by species.

The tallies were carefully recorded to be sent to the Audubon journal, *American Birds*, for publication. There were triumphs and disappointments. One disappointment was that no one spotted a Clapper Rail, an elusive marsh bird that winters along the east coast below Massachusetts. When Brigid expressed her disappointment about the Clapper Rail to the assembled birders, I eagerly volunteered to go out in the dark and cold and try to spot one in a marsh.

How gallant! My good friend Don Wilson—a physicist I'd known for years on Block Island where he had a house—and my loyal son Matt Jr., home for Christmas from college, accompanied me on that quest. We went to a likely marsh and after half an hour neither saw nor heard a Clapper Rail. Returning home we announced our failure to the assembled birders. But my wife seemed pleased by my effort. Perhaps she would ask me to come back with her and the kids to the NYU apartment. But she did not.

She and all the others departed the next day. I stayed on a few more days alone. Taking down our large Christmas tree, each ornament, especially the homemade ones made by my wife and the kids, dredged up happy memories. I cried, thinking of my future life alone.

In March, 1982, I was in my fifth short-term rental. It was a one room (no kitchen) apartment in the East Village that I found, not Sam. I rented it by the week. Each day I had breakfast and dinner at the Kiev, a Ukrainian restaurant on 2nd Avenue. Dinner was usually late because most of my NYU classes were in the evening and most often was pea soup and a cheeseburger. Breakfast was always eggs, bacon, and toast.

My restaurant choice and menu reflect that I was financially strapped by alimony and child support. The East Village was not chic back in 1982. It was mostly Ukrainians and young punk rockers. After dinner I would go to a bar on East 7th Street. Down a few steps from the street, the bar was old and funky. A pay phone with a folding door was next to the bar, and across the way was a 1950s vintage jukebox. The music selection was a mix of the Sex Pistols and Ukrainian marches. The clientele were old Ukrainian men and punk rockers and in the back Ukrainian men and punk rockers amiably shot pool together. In that neighborhood I learned how to distinguish American girls from Ukrainian girls: The Ukrainian girls were invariably blond. The American girls had purple, maroon, or green hair.

In May of 1982, I was still in the short-term rental in the East Village, walking distance from my NYU apartment where my ex-wife and my daughter Maureen continued to live. I visited them one weekend morning to take Maureen out for the day. Standing in the living room staring at the kitchen I thought to myself, *Wouldn't it be nice to have a refrigerator in my one room?* No bitterness, no self-pity, just a simple wish.

My former wife interrupted my silent reverie. "If you don't get NYU to give us a nicer apartment, I'll kill myself!"

Snap. I did not reply. It was then over for me. The grim dark duty of my Catholic upbringing was lifted like a millstone around my neck. That evening I phoned an unmarried woman I was friendly with at W. R. Grace and invited her to have dinner with me.

One ugly burden I had long-carried was a seething anger against rising street crime. I was an enthusiastic supporter of tougher criminal sentences. I had been mugged once, losing only money. Many times I had been aggressively accosted by beggars but never gave them a nickel.

Suddenly that ugly burden vanished. When I noticed it was gone, I thought, *I was really angry at my wife all those years, not street criminals and beggars. But I would not admit it to myself because of my grim Catholic duty.*

A few weeks later I called my truly ex-wife to arrange care of Maureen while I went off to Block Island. "Brigid, I've decided to rent out our Block Island house this summer because I need the money. I've got to go there and get it ready for renters, plus arrange for a broker to list it. So I can't take Maureen out this Saturday or Sunday."

"I'll go with you to help out," she said cheerfully. "We can take Maureen too."

"No, I don't want you to come." Her tone shifted from cheerful to angry. I don't remember what she said, but I was clearly rejecting her company. I had never done that before.

I began to see unattached women who I found appealing. All of them I knew professionally. I did not go to singles bars hoping to hook up with some attractive woman for the night. That impersonal sex was erotically appealing but not emotionally. Besides, I was far too shy to hit on a stranger.

One day in June I ran into my former colleague at NYU, Nora, who was then at another university. I liked her very much, but she had a serious attachment. I invited her to have lunch with me the next week. At lunch she told me that she and her boyfriend were going off to Smith College for the summer where she would be teaching. Would I like to rent her Brooklyn apartment in their absence? Is the Pope Catholic? I was still living in that one room in the East Village. A whole apartment for two months, with a refrigerator too! Her apartment was in the old Ex Lax building on Atlantic Avenue in Boerum Hill, Brooklyn.

Twice in my life I had been in Brooklyn. In 1961, Brigid and I visited a college friend and his wife who were living in a brownstone. Their young landlords owned the house and lived downstairs. We all visited together. The landlady said to me, "Where d'ya live Matt?"

"We live in Inwood in Manhattan," I replied.

"Oh, da city. We was dere once on our honeymoon," she said. I calculated they lived about six or seven subway stops from Times Square.

The second time was in the autumn of 1968. Driving in our Volkswagen Bug near Delancey Street, we made a wrong turn and ended up on the Williamsburg Bridge, which leads to Williamsburg, Brooklyn. It was Friday afternoon and the sidewalks were packed with Hasidim carrying bundles of sticks. Women with three to five children in tow also carried bundles of sticks. We were mystified. A Jewish neighbor later enlightened us about the holiday of Sukkot when orthodox Jews build small sheds with wooden branches.

In early July I left my East Village rented room and moved into Nora's apartment. There were screens on the windows. Living in Greenwich Village since 1972, I had forgotten about screens. Flying insects were rare in the Village but apparently plentiful in Brooklyn.

Three huge windows overlooked Atlantic Avenue, but they were filthy. The first week I spent half a day washing all the windows. A labor of love perhaps. I was quite pleased with the outcome.

One night early on in my stay, I went to a busy Chinese restaurant. While waiting to pay the cashier, a young woman in front of me had a takeout order. She handed the cashier, clearly the owner, a credit card. "No cards," he said matter-of-factly.

"Oh, can I give you a check?" she said with some distress.

"No checks," he answered with no apology or explanation.

Then with more distress she protested. "But I don't have enough cash with me to pay!"

In the same matter-of-fact tone he said, "Come in tomorrow and pay."

She gushed gratitude to him, promised to pay tomorrow, asked if he wanted her phone number and address as some type of security. He repeated "Come in tomorrow and pay." She grabbed her take-out bags and departed. *So, this is Brooklyn,* I thought. It was an unimaginable scene for a Manhattan restaurant.

That summer I was teaching summer school two nights at NYU. I learned to navigate the subway in Brooklyn. Mornings on my way to my NYU office, I walked up to Flatbush Avenue and took the D train to the Broadway-Lafayette stop. At night, returning around 10 p.m., I always took the A train to the Hoyt-Schermerhorn stop because it was a much closer walk (really a run) to the Ex Lax building. Street crime was still rampant in Boerum Hill back then.

I wrote my ex-wife a long letter cataloguing complaints about her, complaints I had not expressed while we were married. I remember the last sentence: "All the friends and relatives in your life still like you, except me." She wrote me a self-flagellating reply. Yes, she was a terrible person and fully deserved my scorn. I did not reply. In retrospect my letter was cowardly. My complaints about her should have been expressed face-to-face. But I knew back then that when I did complain to her about her actions, she quickly escalated to threats of suicide. So I did not bring them up. That was an excuse more than a reason. She had never attempted suicide despite her many threats.

I left Nora's apartment at the end of August when she returned and got a short-term rental from an NYU professor who owned a coop in a high rise in Brooklyn Heights. She said that if asked by tenants what was our connection I must say that we are related because short-term rentals were not permitted. My first day there I ran into one of her neighbors who asked how I was connected with the owner. "I am her cousin," I said.

She replied earnestly, "Oh, you look just like her!"

Shortly after moving in, I got a call from my ex-wife announcing that I *must* take Maureen for a long weekend; my ex had to attend an out-of-town conference. She was an editor at a non-profit organization. Of course, I agreed to take my daughter. When I related that to Nora, she asked if my ex knew that it was a one-bedroom apartment with one bed. "No, she doesn't."

"Why didn't you tell her?"

"It never occurred to me. We'll manage," I said.

"Well if I were Maureen's mother I would *insist* there was a bed for her! What's wrong with your ex? Look, you give Maureen the bedroom and you sleep on the couch. Do you have sheets and pillows for two beds?"

"No, I hadn't thought of that."

"I'll lend you some."

Nora's strong reaction to the imperious behavior of my ex gave me an insight that made me dislike the mother of my children even more. Here, the woman I had been devoted to for two decades had cast me aside like an old worn shoe. I had always been trying, been praying, to be a better husband. I felt cheated by my religious devotion. It had not saved my marriage.

I stopped attending Sunday Mass. More important, I stopped wanting to save my marriage. Devout Catholics in terrible marriages will often seek annulments by the Church, a long and expensive process. If successful, the pleader can resume receiving sacraments and can remarry in the Catholic Church. Just like a reformation zealot, I did not want or need the intervention of clergy to remove the millstone of my marriage from my neck.

Chapter Nineteen

Westbeth, Kathy and Remarriage

Sam told me that his good friend, Toby Schoenbaum, an anthropologist, was going to New Guinea for a few months. "Matt, do you want to rent his apartment? It's in Westbeth in the West Village, a city-owned building on the Hudson, with low rents for artists. You need to get a letter from someone who can say you're an artist."

"What's Toby's claim as an artist?"

"He published a book on Peru, *Keep the River on Your Right.*"

So I easily got the necessary letter, met Toby, toured his studio apartment, and I was in. The one requirement that Toby insisted upon was that once a week I watered all the plants. There was a dense profusion of plants hanging from the fourteen-foot ceiling all along the banks of windows facing the Hudson River. Toby had a step ladder necessary for the task. Every Saturday morning I watered the plants. It took almost three hours. The walls were hung with New Guinea and Peruvian treasures: masks, swords, armor. I lived there from October 1982 to May 1983.

Westbeth was walking distance from NYU, and the apartment was on the sixth floor. One night I was awakened by a stream of bright lights moving along the Hudson River at eye level. I ran over to a window to see. It was a brightly lit ocean liner steaming by, maybe a cruise ship headed for Europe.

Early on in my Westbeth stay, I arranged a dinner with my two kids, Nora, and one of my nephews from Detroit who was staying with me while he searched for a job and apartment in New York. We all met at an Indian restaurant in the East Village that I frequented when I lived there. Matt Jr. was home from college in Maine and staying with his mother and Maureen in our NYU apartment.

Even though Nora was not my girlfriend, I think I wanted my kids to believe that perhaps she was so they wouldn't think, "Poor Dad is all alone." Better yet, they might convey to their mother that I was "seeing" someone. It was a jolly evening. After dinner my kids returned to the NYU apartment while my nephew and I walked to Westbeth. Less than an hour after our return, Maureen and Matt Jr. showed up at my apartment. Maureen had been there with me some weekends and so knew where it was. Brigid had thrown them out when she learned that they had been to dinner with me and some woman, angry that she had not been invited! That is what they told me, and I believed them. So I got them blankets, gave my bed to Maureen, slept on the couch, and Matt Jr. and my nephew slept on the floor. At my NYU office the next day I got a call from our long-standing cleaning lady who tearfully explained, "Oh Matt, your wife is in bed crying so much! Please come over!" My ex was no doubt remorseful about kicking her children out the night before. But she was no longer my problem. I called Matt Jr. still at Westbeth and told him, and he went to his mother.

One weekend night in November, my ex called me in Toby's apartment, all sweetness and light, inviting me to come over. She could be very persuasive, but I declined her invitation. After hanging up, I rushed out of the apartment and went to a nearby jazz bar for the rest of the evening, fearing she would call back and I would succumb to her invitation.

On December 2, 1982, I met my future wife.

I had arranged a dinner meeting with Nora at her office. When I arrived I was surprised to see another woman there who I did not know, Kathy Stone. It was clear by her glum expression that she was not happy about my inclusion in this event. Nora apologized to both of us for having mistakenly made these two separate dates for the same night.

I had first heard about Kathy from Nora a few months before. "She is really brilliant, a Harvard Law School graduate who has published an article in the *Yale Law Review*," Nora had said. "She works at the famous Rabinowitz and Boudin law firm. But I suspect she wants to become a law professor. Someday she will probably be a star legal scholar. You should meet her."

I replied, "You know my requirements for a serious girlfriend are she must smoke, and she must have children, because I'm not about to become a father again."

"She smokes, but has no children" Nora said. "She's never been married." (I had smoked a pipe then switched to cigarettes; Kathy smoked at the time but later we both gave it up—she for good and me more than once. As Mark Twain said, "Giving up smoking is the easiest thing in the world. I know because I've done it thousands of times.")

We all went out to a nearby restaurant. I remember talking about birding, Block Island, and comparing childhood summer experiences, Kathy's on Cape Cod, mine on the Great Lakes, and Nora's at summer camp near Pittsburg. Kathy talked about her civil rights work at the law firm, and her Yale publication. I talked about my NYU career. Her glum expression had disappeared, replaced by warm smiles and laughter that made her so pretty. I was smitten.

After dinner we all took the subway to Brooklyn, getting off at Kathy's stop near Cobble Hill. She and Nora wanted to show me Kathy's apartment. It was the full first floor of a brownstone with twelve-foot ceilings and handsome wooden parquet floors. Near the top of the living room walls were plaster Greco-Roman busts about every four feet. A grand marble fireplace enhanced the room. Double-sliding wooden doors separated the living room from the bedroom. Nora, having visited there before, stayed in the living room while Kathy showed me the rest of the apartment. When we stepped into the large closet, I had a strong urge to kiss her. Always shy and never bold, I resisted that desire. We said our goodbyes, and I walked Nora to her Ex Lax building a few blocks away. On the walk there I said, "Was that a plot of yours to get me together with Kathy?"

"Oh, you know me. I often screw up appointments." That was true, but I had my doubts. Nora probably found me needy of her company, which I was, and her serious boyfriend who lived in Washington, D.C. might be jealous.

With Christmas around the corner, I had arranged with my ex a Block Island plan. She would take the kids there for Christmas and the annual Christmas Bird Count scheduled for December 23, and then return alone to New York the day after Christmas. I would show up that evening to spend holiday time with them. I was determined to do a second *better* Christmas December 27, with presents, a turkey dinner, and a surprise guest, Matt Jr.'s best friend Brian Wilson. I had spent the December 25 Christmas at the home of the Wilsons in New Jersey. The next day, Brian and I drove to Block Island.

On the second Christmas eve, after Maureen had gone to sleep, the three of us worked feverishly building and decorating a small doll house for her. We had a grand Christmas day December 27 with stocking treats, presents, eggnogs, and of course I cooked a fine turkey dinner. There was one mishap. I spilled a whole pan of carefully prepared turkey gravy on the kitchen floor, a floor that was stupidly carpeted by the previous owner and builder.

Matt Jr., Maureen, and Brian returned to New York a few days later. I stayed on through New Year's Day, taking down the Christmas tree that the kids had decorated with their mother. No tears this time.

For years I had wanted to circumnavigate Block Island on the beach, about a twelve-mile walk. My ex wanted to do it with me, but something always came up so we never did it. Now in early January 1983 I decided to walk it alone, or at least half of it. The Great Salt Pond in the middle of the island presented a barrier as it had a cut opening it to the ocean. So I began my walk in town, walking south along the beach until I reached the cut, and then headed back home. It was a gorgeous winter day; bright blue sky with fluffy white clouds. The temperature was above freezing. Block Island's climate is moderated by the surrounding ocean.

Along my walk I thought about Kathy. I wanted to call her and invite her out to dinner as soon as I returned to New York. She was smart and lovely and fun to talk with. But one thing might lead to another, and Kathy, twelve years younger than me, probably wanted to have children. Casual sex was not appealing to me. So what should I do? Remembering how happy I was with my two kids at Christmas, I realized that I could be happy again with a new child. All of that was going through my mind as I trudged along the sand that day.

I knew I was a good father. My children loved me. I could be a good father to another child. So, I decided to call and ask her out. It might lead to nothing, but I was willing to risk that. Almost two years later, in October 1984, Kathy and I were married at her mother's house in Georgetown. Nora and my good friend Don Wilson from Block Island spoke at our wedding.

Nora related the story of how her bungling appointments first brought Kathy and I together. I still had my doubts about her story. But I was happy with the outcome.

Indeed I was, and after more than three decades of marriage I am very happy with our life together. Kathy is a wonderful wife, As I age, I depend on her even more than before. She supports me cheerfully, and I cannot imagine being without her. She accepts all of my friends, and they are quite fond of her. We have a great social life, hosting many lively dinner parties and attending as guests to friends' parties. When I first met Kathy, I was a tenured professor at the Wagner School, NYU. I thought I would remain there the rest of my professional life. But thanks to her, we moved first to Cornell and then to UCLA. She was a star, I was not. As better offers came to her, she always insisted that I be hired as well, and I was.

On social issues Kathy and I agreed. We clashed on major economic issues. She had been a labor historian and was by then a professor of labor law. She was well known on the left as a supporter of unions. Her article "Job Structures in the Steel Industry," first published in 1974, cemented her reputation. Her article was widely known outside the legal profession and had been translated into several languages. More than once at academic conferences, I was introduced as Katherine Stone's husband, ". . . you know, the author of 'Job Structures in the Steel Industry.'" The left-leaning academics always knew her and were impressed.

But I was a strongly empirical economist. The fact that the growth in average real wages over the twentieth century tracked the growth in productivity (real output per worker), both *before* the rise of unionization and *after*, convinced me that unions had *nothing* to do with real wage growth. So we argued about that. To convince her that I was right, I updated that graph with the latest U.S. Department of Labor data on productivity and real wages. But, to my shock the data starting in 1979 showed a divergence, with productivity continuing to rise while real wages became stagnant. And that divergence was no temporary blip. It continues to this day. But what do unions have to do with that divergence? A lot, I believe now. The peak in U.S. unionization was thirty percent in 1960. Now it is under ten percent in the private sector. That means the power of labor is diminished. The only power neoclassical economics recognizes is that of impersonal markets, and that is a big mistake.

Chapter Twenty

Our Brooklyn Brownstone in Park Slope

Kathy and I lived in her Cobble Hill Brooklyn apartment after our wedding. All through 1985 we searched for a larger apartment to buy in Brooklyn. Manhattan was out of the question because the real estate prices were much higher than Brooklyn back then. Both of us worked in Greenwich Village in Manhattan, me at NYU and she at Cardozo Law School. Appealing Brooklyn neighborhoods—Cobble Hill, Brooklyn Heights, and Park Slope—were short subway rides from Greenwich Village, so that's where we concentrated our search. We probably toured two dozen apartments and houses, some more than once.

We made an offer on a beautiful old three-story frame house in Park Slope, contingent on an engineer inspection. The engineer discovered that the main supporting beam in the cellar was heavily infested with termites, so we cancelled our offer.

A floor-through apartment of a large brownstone in Brooklyn

Heights that backed up on the Brooklyn Promenade had a spectacular view of lower Manhattan. The novelist Norman Mailer lived upstairs. It was beyond our price range.

Then we found it. A four-story brownstone on a street only one block long, walking distance to the grand Prospect Park, the park that Olmstead "got right" as its admirers claimed. The entire house was occupied by one family. It had never been converted to tiny rental units during the World War II housing crunch in New York City. The kitchen was on the garden floor. A dumb waiter connected it to the dining room on the first floor. We fell in love with that house. If we converted the garden floor into a rental unit (it had a separate entrance under the stoop), then we could afford it. Of course, we would need to add a kitchen to the first floor, which was majestic: twelve-foot ceilings, a marble fireplace, dark mahogany paneling with matching sliding doors, stained glass windows in the entrance way. We paid $425,000 for it in 1985. Neighbors noted our purchase price in hushed tones—no house on that block had ever sold for over $400,000! Some years later when we were living in Ithaca, Kathy learned that a floor-through apartment on that block in Park Slope sold for $500,000.

Our realtor connected us with a good contractor, Craig Hoffheimer, who could do the changes we needed to convert the garden floor to a rental apartment, install a kitchen on the first floor, and build a deck overlooking our back yard. He did not do electrical work or plumbing, so we found others to do that. The garden floor needed a shower to convert its half-bath to a full bathroom. I came home as the plumber was finishing up that job and was horrified to see that he made the shower door open into the kitchen, not into the bathroom. I tried not to laugh or cry as I pointed out that major flaw to him. He saw nothing wrong with such an arrangement, but was happy to please an overly fastidious client. So he fixed it.

The two electricians we hired had day jobs at a huge warehouse, and they moonlighted doing small electrical jobs. They did some rewiring and installed light switches. Again I arrived just as they were finishing up and discovered that all of the light switches they put in were crooked. I said, "Ed, all the light switches are crooked."

Good naturedly he replied, "Oh, you wanted them straight?" I assured him that I did, and thought probably no one at a warehouse cares if the light switches are straight or not.

The shower and the light switch problems were easy to solve. The deck construction problem was not. Kathy and I conferred with Craig about the deck design and steps going down to the yard. It would be the same width as the house, about sixteen feet, and extending over the yard about eight feet. In building the deck, Craig and his helpers ran a nail or two into the side of the house next door. The two elderly sisters who lived there reported our extravagant violation of their property to the building department. They persuaded an inspector to come out and investigate. He apparently was indifferent to the offending nails, but he filed a violation by us for building a deck without a permit.

Thus, we were then caught up in the Byzantine world of the New York City building department. Our first response was to discuss with a building department expert how to deal with our violation. As an attorney, my wife Kathy sensibly asked to see the building code. He smiled broadly, throwing his hands in the air and replied, "The code is an oral tradition."

Our next response was to hire a real estate lawyer who was savvy about building department rules. He told us to apply for a permit as if the deck was not built yet. He said both sides to a dispute benefitted from that fiction, why I cannot say. We paid the requisite fee, and filled out the permit, which required providing dimensions of the deck-to-be. Our lawyer provided those numbers, never having seen or measured the real deck already built, but knowing the dimensions that the building department required for approval. We did measure the real deck and found that it was two feet wider than what the building department would approve. How would they ever know that discrepancy? Easy—they would send one of their building inspectors to see the finished deck. Our final hurdle was to somehow persuade the inspector that the actual deck was indeed in compliance with the required measures, provided by our savvy lawyer, noted in the building permit.

Once that construction of the deck was "completed" (it had been completed months ago), I was to schedule an inspection with the building department. With my calendar book in hand, I appeared at their office to schedule an appointment for the inspection. They gave me a number of optional dates in the near future. Looking at their choice of dates, I noted that one of them was a major Jewish holiday. *Perfect*, I thought to myself. *Building inspector is a cushy job in Brooklyn, so their number probably consists of long-time white residents who are Irish, Italian, or Jewish.* My stereotypes of those three ethnic groups was that the Jews were more likely to go by the rules while the Irish and Italian were more likely to bend the rules. If they liked you. So I picked the Jewish holiday for my inspection date, believing that Jewish inspectors would not be working that day.

Craig gave me another idea for passing inspection that I never thought of: intimidation. Craig had a friend with two Doberman Pinschers who sometimes rented them out to someone who felt threatened. He lived nearby. I went to his home to meet him and the dogs. "The mother," he explained, "will wander in your yard and not pay much attention to you. The young dog will stand on the deck, eager for attention." Both dogs were similar in size.

"I want the young dog." I said without hesitation. We agreed on a price and the date. He would bring the young dog over to me early in the morning.

On the appointed day for my deck inspection, the dog's owner delivered him and set him loose on the deck. I had donned my outfit for the inspector's visit: a Loyola sweatshirt of my son's and khaki pants. The inspector arrived around 10 a.m. His name was Dominic Bonomollo. We sat in the dining room with a glass door opening onto the deck as Dominic filled out some official form. All the while, the young dog was staring at us from the other side of the door. When Dominic finished with his form, he stood up, walked over to the door, and peeked out at the deck. "Looks okay to me," he said, jotting something down on the form.

* * *

After my divorce, Brigid had custody of Maureen. Matt Jr. was in college. I had to go to court to win visiting rights over Maureen, which I did, because Brigid only allowed me visits at her convenience or when she was going out of town. Brigid and Maureen were then living in Larchmont because NYU revoked my lease when they learned that I no longer lived in the NYU apartment. Maureen attended the Larchmont high school and Brigid commuted from Larchmont to her job in New York City.

One evening when Maureen, then a freshman in high school, and Brigid were dining near Grand Central Station before returning to Larchmont by train, Maureen piped up cheerfully, "What would you think if I lived with Dad and Kathy for a while?"

Brigid immediately replied angrily, "If you did that, you would never see me again!" She grabbed her coat and marched out of the restaurant. Maureen had little money and no train ticket, so she called me in Brooklyn. I told her to get a cab and come to our house, which she did. Before Maureen arrived, Brigid called and demanded that I send Maureen back to her at Grand Central. My wife, the attorney, said I had to comply because Brigid had custody, not me. Maureen was crestfallen when I told her, but she did not resist. I gave her money for the cab and helped her hail one. It turned out to be the same cab she had arrived in.

Two years later, when Maureen was a junior in high school,

Brigid kicked her out of the house with all her possessions. Maureen continued to be rebellious in her adolescence, and came to us in Brooklyn. She told me that two weeks before she had once again said, "I want to live with Dad," and Brigid replied firmly "Over my dead body!" Apparently Brigid changed her mind.

I got the same lawyer who successfully gained me visit rights for Maureen, and I now wanted custody of Maureen. The lawyer impressed me when he told me his story of winning visit rights for another father. "Judge," he'd said, "here is a phone. Please call Attica prison and ask them what visit rights are granted to their worst prisoner. I will take them for my client."

The court strategy he had for me was to file my petition for custody in Brooklyn Family Court, not Manhattan. "The Brooklyn judges *never* see a father asking for custody, so they will sit up and take sympathetic notice!" I happily won custody of Maureen. When I told two of my older sisters, both of whom had raised teenage daughters, of my court victory, they each had the same response: "Poor Kathy!" They were right. The next months were tumultuous with a rebellious teenage girl in our home.

The first order for me was to get Maureen enrolled in a high school in the middle of the school year. One of my good friends from our years in Putnam Valley was Al Shanker, president of the New York teachers union. I asked for his assistance. He managed to get Maureen into Midwood High School in Brooklyn, one of the city's magnet schools. Most days Maureen skipped school at Midwood, joined up with her deadbeat Larchmont friends, and they hung out in the city. She was in 11th grade and failed with flying colors. The highest grade on her final report card was a C in music.

I had warned her throughout her stay at Midwood that if she did not succeed, I would do something radical. I did. I got her into a Friends boarding school in Maryland, the high school Kathy had attended and loved. Maureen repeated 11th grade there with success, did 12th grade and graduated in June of 1990. She started college the next autumn at SUNY New Paltz. The timing was good because Kathy and I were off to Chicago, where she was a visiting professor at the University of Chicago Law School. We rented out our Brooklyn brownstone while we were away.

Our daughter Erica was born in 1989, more than a year before we departed for Chicago. We were delighted and relieved because Kathy had so many miscarriages before Erica came along. After the last miscarriage, Kathy found a new doctor in Philadelphia who was expert on preventing miscarriages. That doctor discovered that Kathy had an inherited immune system disorder that treated a pregnancy as an invasion by a foreign object. The body's response was to attack by cutting off blood to the fetus. The medical response was to thin the blood by frequent injections of a blood thinner. My job was to administer those shots to her regularly. During that successful pregnancy, we drove to Philadelphia perhaps weekly to meet with that doctor who was carefully monitoring the fetus's condition and development.

Chapter Twenty-One

Cape Cod

I must back up in time now to explain how I went from spending summers on Block Island to spending them on Cape Cod.

To complete my divorce settlement with Brigid, I had to sell my Block Island house in 1984. I was sad about that loss. That summer, Kathy and I rented a house on Block Island for part of August, but it was a disappointment. No ocean views, and a defective steamed up picture window looking out on a pond. In the autumn we rented a charming old house on Block Island where we wrote our wedding vows for our upcoming wedding in October. The next three summers as a married couple we again had one- or two-week rentals on Block Island. In those summers we spent much time searching for a house or a building lot, but to no avail. The prices were too high for us, particularly because we had purchased the brownstone house in Park Slope, Brooklyn in 1985. So, we resigned ourselves to not having a Block Island house.

Then in the summer of 1988 we reached a deal with Kathy's

mother to split the rent for a house in Wellfleet on Cape Cod. She and her husband, David, would take it for one month, we for another, and we would overlap for one week. That first summer I almost ached to be back on Block Island. But my mourning passed and turned to relief and joy in all the following summers, and up to the present, that we have spent on Cape Cod.

I came to like Cape Cod better than Block Island because of the many friends we had there. Some we had originally known in New York City and Boston. Most were academics like us. There were also prominent neoclassical economists there in the summer; none of whom I knew, such as Larry Summers and Robert Barro of Harvard, and Gary Becker of the University of Chicago, now deceased. Two economists I did know and came to like were Barry Bluestone and Bennet Harrison, who is now deceased. They were not neoclassical economists, and they were both strongly empirical, like me.

Long before anyone was writing about income inequality and the decline of labor unions, they co-wrote *The Great U-Turn: Corporate Restructuring and the Polarizing of America* in1990, which addressed those issues. I was still a true believer in neoclassical economics when that book came out, and I did not read it then. The economics profession mostly trashed the book, which explains why I did not read it. Kathy had been friends with Barry and Bennett in Boston, and reunited with them when we started going to Cape Cod in the summer. They both owned summer houses on the Cape. When I finally read their book I liked it. I had changed for the better.

A friend we made on the Cape and saw each summer was John McDermott, a professor at SUNY Old Westbury. He was famous on the left during the Vietnam War for his newsletter, the "Viet Report." Not as famous as I.F. Stone for his weekly Vietnam report, but famous nonetheless. One evening when John and his wife Frindy were visiting, the discussion turned to John Maynard Keynes. I had become disillusioned with Keynes in the 1970s when I was still a true believer in neoclassical economics. That was because during a recession in Europe, France launched a large-scale deficit spending program, a Keynesian policy. That is, France cut taxes so that the government's revenues from taxes were much smaller than government expenditures. Therefore the French deficit, the difference between government revenues and government expenditures, ballooned. It did not stimulate demand for goods and services in France. All it accomplished was a run-up in French imports. I explained that to John, Frindy, and Kathy. They were all appalled that I was disillusioned with Keynes.

But I learned years later that if France had designed the program to boost employment and earnings through infrastructure expenditures, it might have worked. The problem was that France copied U.S. fiscal policy of lowering taxes, believing that that would stimulate consumption. Tax cuts do not raise earnings for those with no earnings, the unemployed. So I was no longer disillusioned with Keynes.

I was disillusioned with neoclassical economists, who always preferred tax cuts to boosting infrastructure spending in a recession.

Massive infrastructure spending by government (i.e. for roads, bridges, airports, water supply systems, etc.) leads to increased employment in construction and industries that are suppliers for construction. Such workers tend to spend all their income rather than save a large part of it. Tax cuts do not help the unemployed.

Chapter Twenty-Two

University of Chicago

In late August of 1990, we moved to Chicago for the fall semester. My wife, Kathy, a law professor at Cardozo Law School in New York, had been offered a visiting professor position at the University of Chicago Law School for the fall. She had eagerly accepted it, as well as a spring visit at the Cornell Law School. Both were highly-ranked law schools, so a permanent offer at either one would advance her academic career.

I supported her strategy for those two appointments. We did not wish to have a long-distance commuting marriage, not with a toddler, and so our hope was that if she received a permanent appointment offer from either of those law schools, I would find a permanent offer in the same metropolitan area, if not in the same university.

I was a tenured professor at NYU. I had negotiated a one-year unpaid academic leave from NYU for 1990–91 so we could go first to Chicago and then to Cornell. I viewed that as a great adventure with no guarantees. I was offered two courses of microeconomics to teach as an adjunct at the University of Chicago, one in the Harris School of Public Policy and one in the School of Social Service Administration, both graduate courses. Despite my growing skepticism about neoclassical economics, I was in awe of the University of Chicago. I remember commenting to friends and my wife once my adjunct position was secured, that I felt like a country priest summoned for a position at the Vatican. It was true.

But like the Vatican, the University of Chicago had serious flaws. It was ironic to me that that foremost bastion of *laissez faire* had transformed its Chicago neighborhood, Hyde Park, into a tightly controlled environment. In his fine book, *The Color of Law* (2018), Richard Rothstein notes:

> "The University of Chicago organized and guided property owners' associations that were devoted to preventing black families from moving nearby. The university not only subsidized the associations but from 1933 to 1947 spent $100,000 on legal services to defend covenants and evict African Americans who had arrived in its neighborhood. When criticized for these activities, University of Chicago president Robert Maynard Hutchins wrote in 1937 that the university 'must endeavor to stabilize its neighborhood as an area in which its students and faculty will be content to live,' and that therefore the university had the 'right to invoke and defend' restrictive covenants in its surrounding areas." (p. 105)

It was not just racial discrimination in housing supported by the University of Chicago but also its control of Urban Renewal spending in Hyde Park. That began in the 1950s. As the great migration of post-World War II poured hundreds of thousands of rural black southerners into Chicago, the south side of that city emptied of whites and filled with blacks. Hyde Park is deep on the south side. Some University of Chicago faculty and students were pushing for a move out of Chicago to a suburb. But the university administration decided to stay in Hyde Park.

Julian Levi, founder and head of the South East Chicago Commission (SECC), put together an urban renewal plan for Hyde Park that reflected the goals of the university. Levi's brother, Edward, was the Dean of the Law School at the time. In 1958, Chicago's Mayor Daley approved the SECC plan. Urban Renewal was a federal program that funded massive demolition of "slums" and new construction in the 1950s and 1960s. The University of Chicago got to influence urban renewal spending in Hyde Park. A lively nightlife scene of bars and music at 59th Street in Hyde Park was essentially shut down. During my stay, there was one seedy bar remaining on 59th Street, the only one in Hyde Park. Traffic patterns discouraged access to Hyde Park from the north or the south. There was one movie theater and one supermarket and few restaurants.

The effect was to discourage visitors other than those going to the University of Chicago. The university's police force was purportedly one of the largest private police operations in the nation. Urban renewal brought high-rise, low-income housing to central cities, but not to Hyde Park. That history of the University of Chicago's active intervention to make Hyde Park a "planned" neighborhood by a university contemptuous of urban planning is not well known.

When we arrived in Chicago that September, our daughter was almost one-and-a-half years old and spoke in cogent two-word sentences. Walking up the sidewalk to the rental house with her early on in our stay, she said, "New home."

Visiting a cousin who taught music at a Chicago middle school, little Erica joined her in the kitchen where she was cooking and listening to some symphonic music on the radio. My cousin was bowled over when Erica said "Mahler."

As our stay in Chicago was extended, so did Erica's vocabulary. One day, as we were driving up Lakeside Drive, Erica, from her car seat, said, "I like to see the lake." Six words!

The law school was noted as a center of the law and economics movement. Each week they had a guest speaker. The always large audience was dominated by the famous scholars Richard Posner, a federal judge, Richard Epstein and Frank Esterbrook, both Chicago Law School faculty. For the weekly session that I attended, the speaker was a liberal from Northwestern Law School. He was addressing the issue of legal remedies for negative externalities. (A negative externality in economics is a spillover from producers or consumers that injures the welfare of others not involved. For example, the burning of coal to produce steel spreads hazardous smoke well beyond the area of the steel plant.)

Someone in the audience piped up dismissively, "Oh, we considered that a few years ago." Old. Stale.

The speaker smiled nervously and asked, "Well, what did you conclude?"

"No legal remedies are required. The market can deal efficiently with externalities." Amen, the audience chimed in.

The speaker objected. "But how can the market deal with all the coal dust of daily coal shipments from West Virginia to the port of Baltimore, dust that blankets residences and businesses and schools?"

"Oh, let me answer!" shouted Richard Epstein, waving his arm frantically to Esterbrook, the moderator. Without waiting for a nod of ascent, Epstein said, "All of the property owners along the route of the train have the cost of the externalities capitalized into the value of their real estate. Being perfectly rational, they knew that when they purchased the property."

"Maybe that is so for the commercial property owners, but what about the households, the home owners, and the school districts?"

"Those agents are rational too. If they are 'surprised' by the daily blankets of coal dust, they must be stupid, or what is he same thing, liberal," Epstein retorted, and the audience laughed.

The speaker responded, "It is public knowledge that daily exposure to coal dust constitutes a health hazard. All those public school children in the path of the coal trains are at risk."

Epstein replied, "In a world of perfect information, their parents knew that risk, and chose to take it."

"Would you take it for your kids?"

"Of course not! I am always rational!"

And so it continued with other audience members jumping in to support Epstein's argument.

I remarked to someone how hard the audience was on the speaker. "Oh, did you think so? I didn't. The only rule observed at these events is to not attack the speaker until *after* their introduction by the moderator."

In the first week of classes that semester, I gave my list of proposed office hours to the secretary. The class had fifty students and met twice a week, so I proposed four hours per week. She looked aghast at my proposal, and whispered, "Don't do that! No one does that!" *Who am I to rock this boat?* I thought. I cut back to two hours per week.

My microeconomics class of Harris Public Policy School had, hands-down, the best students I have ever taught. They seemed to have done heavier reading I assigned than the NYU students, asked better questions, and earned higher grades. Better than NYU, better than Cornell, and better than UCLA. Just as at Cornell and UCLA, all of the Harris School graduate students were full-time.

The reason I was offered the adjunct position teaching microeconomics at the Harris School is that the economics faculty member who taught it was on leave as a visitor at a competing economics department that fall. He was young, brilliant, and had turned lots of heads in the profession. Years later he, James Heckman, was awarded the Nobel Memorial Prize in Economics for his econometrics work that established a superior way to analyze large samples of people without introducing bias. His econometric method spread to other social sciences that deal with large samples of people.

My other course at Chicago that term was also microeconomics, teaching graduate students in the School of Social Service Administration. It was an evening course because most of those students were part-time. I taught a less rigorous version than I did at the Harris School. The class was in the Social Service Administration building located on the south side of East 60th Street, the south end of the campus.

One night in the middle of my lecture, two Chicago policemen appeared at my open door and motioned for me to come over. Could they ask my class about a very recent incident outdoors? Yes, of course I responded. They came in and one of them said to the class, "Hey, we got a dead body out in back, probably a drug deal gone bad. Did any of you hear something?" Some students nodded yes. One volunteered she heard shots just before class began. Then the police left. We all rushed over to the windows in the back of the first-floor classroom. We saw a stretcher with a blanket covering someone whose sneakers stuck out the back. Behind the building was an expansive grassy area, the south boundary of the campus. Police carried the stretcher out of the field.

I resumed my lecture. The next morning, I scanned the campus newspaper and the *Chicago Tribune* for a report on the fatal shooting.

Nothing. *Well, maybe tomorrow,* I thought. But again, there was no news about that event. Perhaps the long arm of the University of Chicago kept such events out of the local newspapers.

Always on the alert for possible jobs in Chicago, I connected with economists at the Federal Reserve Bank of Chicago, attending their semi-weekly talks. They were right up my alley: very empirical and very focused on urban issues. As they became accustomed to my regular attendance, some of them remarked, "You are the only economist from the University of Chicago who has ever come to our events." Often in attendance were academic economists from other universities, such as Northwestern, University of Illinois, Chicago, and even faraway University of Illinois, Urbana. One from U. of Illinois, Chicago whom I became friendly with invited me for lunch one day and asked me about the University of Chicago Law School. When I told him about their weekly faculty lunch everyone was expected to attend, he gasped, "What circle of hell was that invented in?"

The only urban economist in the University of Chicago economics department when I was there was George Tolley, and we became friendly. I taught his undergraduate urban economics course once when he was away. Urban economics is not what Paul Krugman would call a "flagship field" of economics departments. Consequently, I had the impression that Tolley was not part of the inner circle of stars there.

* * *

An unforgettable shocking event for me was an encounter on an elevator. I was departing from a talk at the economics department. There were three other men on the elevator, none known to me. One of them was bragging about sexual exploits on campus. "Sometimes around lunchtime, one of us would pair up with one of the secretaries and retreat to our parked car for a quick screw." He smiled and his listeners laughed. I was appalled that he would relate that incident with a stranger, me, in the elevator. For all he and his listeners knew, I could be the spouse or the son of a secretary who worked there. I would be saddled forever with painful doubts about my wife's or my mother's faithfulness. I wanted to say that on the spot, but timidly remained silent.

The only memento I brought away from our stay is a tee shirt listing all the University of Chicago Nobel prize winners. The list is long, but I would quibble with some of those economists claimed for Chicago. Paul Samuelson is on the list, but he was never on the Chicago economics faculty. Perhaps he was a visiting professor once or an undergraduate.

A few days after New Year's Day, 1991, Kathy and I packed up for the trip to Ithaca to begin our spring semester visits on the faculty of Cornell; she in the law school, me in urban planning. After Erica was in bed, we undecorated the Christmas tree, put it in the trash, and packed away the toys and gifts. When Erica awoke the next day, she came down the stairs and noticed much was missing. She then said anxiously, "Santa, come back soon!"

My wife, a noted scholar of labor law, was not offered a

permanent faculty position by the University of Chicago Law School. Dominated as it was by law and economics professors, we were not surprised. On to the next adventure.

Chapter Twenty-Three

Cornell

In January 1991 we moved from Chicago to Cornell in Ithaca, New York. My wife was at the law school, and I was at the department of City and Regional Planning. We rented a house for the spring semester that was within walking distance to the campus. Before the end of that semester my wife was offered a tenured professor position at the Cornell Law School. I was voted an appointment in planning, but no "line," vacant position, was available in that department. So the deans worked out a complicated deal with NYU, whereby I would teach full-time in the fall at NYU and full-time in the spring at Cornell until a line opened up in City and Regional Planning. Then I would become a full-time tenured professor there. A line did open up in my third year of commuting to NYU in the fall, so I retired from NYU and was appointed at Cornell.

Near the end of my years at NYU, I realized that all of my professional publications, the basis for an academic reputation, were about New York. That was a big mistake. I was a big fish in a local pond. I was determined to change that while remaining an urban and regional economist. That is, I would not just write about New York. And I would focus on getting my articles published in *refereed* journals, the gold standard for economists. A refereed journal uses a double blind method of selecting submitted articles for publication. That is, the author's name is not revealed to the three reviewers given the article, and the reviewers' names are not revealed to the author.

In the thirteen years from 1979 through 1992 I published thirteen articles about the New York City and regional economy in thirteen edited books. Five of them were in the annual book, *Setting Municipal Priorities*. Those were all entitled "The Local Economy and Local [Tax] Revenues." In the article "The Internationalization of New York," I explained how many foreign firms (banks, other financial firms) had opened branches in New York City. At the same time, many New York producer service firms, particularly banks and law firms, opened branches abroad, mostly in London.

In another article, "New York Airline Industry Flies High," I covered the expansion of air service in the city and its economic impact. Ditto for health services ("Health Sector's Significance For New York City Economy"). One favorite article, "The Apple's Core: New York City's Export Industries," explicitly identified the industries in New York that drove the city's economy, mostly producer service industries. A theme that is in all those articles is that the drastic shrinkage of manufacturing in New York did *not* cripple the economy as it did in so many rustbelt cities.

In that same period, I published only three articles in refereed journals, and all of them were about New York. As the humor magazine, *The Onion*, observed post-9/11, the world was *temporarily* interested in and sympathetic with New York. I realized that I had to move on and write about other urban areas.

The first refereed article I published that was *not* just about New York came out in 1989 while I was still at NYU. It was about producer services industries, sometimes called "information intensive industries," in large metropolitan areas of the United States. I had been focused on such industries in New York since publishing the *Corporate Headquarters Complex* in 1977. The argument was that the concentration of such industries enhanced economic growth in large metropolitan areas.

The themes that I wrote about when I mostly stopped writing about New York were attacking neoclassical economics assumptions about states and urban areas. One of those is income convergence. The neoclassical position is that states' personal incomes are indeed variable, but that over the decades they are converging because rational workers move from low-wage states to high-wage states, and rational firms move from low-profit states (where wages are high) to high-profit states (where wages are low). Wages gradually rise as workers move out and profits gradually fall as new firms move in. Thus long-run convergence occurs.

For decades, back to the 1870s, the state data mostly supported convergence of personal income across states. But convergence became divergence in the 1920s before convergence resumed in the 1930s, and convergence was replaced by divergence in the 1980s. Personal incomes continue to diverge to this day in 2021.

How does convergence shift to become divergence? Some states and metropolitan areas have long-term economic booms because their economies are specialized in rapidly growing industries (producer services and health care). Some states and metropolitan areas have long-term economic slumps because their economies are specialized in declining or stagnant industries (agriculture and manufacturing). So, over time, personal income grows faster in the booming places and slower, or hardly at all, in places with economic slumps.

The first problem with that neoclassical position is that states are not the right unit of analysis because a state is not a single labor market. The correct units are metropolitan areas. Recent analyses, including my own, use metropolitan areas. Such data were not available in the distant past. The second problem with that position is that it ignores rising income inequality that we have had in the United States since the 1980s (and back in the 1920s too). In 1980, the top one percent of U.S. households received ten percent of all income. By 2016, the top one percent received more than twenty percent of all income. So, the bottom ninety-nine percent went from getting ninety percent of all income in 1980 to less than eighty percent in 2016. It is no wonder to me that Trump got elected in 2016.

From 1996 to 2005, I published four refereed articles criticizing the neoclassical position supporting income convergence. Also in that period, I published a book, *The Information Economy and American Cities*, in 2002. In it, I attacked the popular idea that sun-belt cities were doing fine economically while snow-belt cities were not. I showed that cities that specialized in the information industries (mostly producer service industries), such as Boston, were doing very well economically while sun-belt cities, such as Los Angeles, were not.

The faculty in my department at Cornell consisted mostly of Marxists and aging hippies. Some were both. They were all friendly to me, but because of my economics Ph.D. I was viewed with suspicion. At NYU my political reputation was as a fiscal conservative and a social liberal. Here, I was considered to the right of Milton Friedman. One faculty member was reported to have had a huge portrait of Mao Tse-tung on his office wall. He took it down when he was made chair of the department and was frequently visited by the provost.

Academic incest was rampant in the department. Five of the nine senior faculty had won their Ph.D.s from that department. One of the four exceptions, Barclay Jones, had been instrumental in hiring those five former Ph.D. students. Oddly enough, Barclay was neither a Marxist nor an aging hippie. He was a Republican. He was also a smoker. Smoking was forbidden in our building, Sibley Hall. But Barclay had a dispensation from that rule. His office reeked of cigarettes. He kept odd hours. Never arriving before 10 a.m., and leaving around midnight except when he kept one of his Ph.D. students much longer. I sometimes saw a forlorn student waiting in a folding chair outside Barclay's office late at night. His meetings with his Ph.D. students were never short because he most carefully read their dissertation chapter drafts. Errors of substance, grammar, and spelling were marked for correction, some of his students told me.

Barclay liked me because I was an economist. One day as we chatted in his smoke-filled office, the topic of peer reviewed articles came up. When I asked his opinion as to what journal I might submit my latest article, he said dismissively, "Oh, I never bother with peer review journals. I have all my articles printed by an excellent service here in Ithaca." I was stunned. The reputation of any economist rests upon articles published in peer-reviewed journals, especially the leading ones. He yanked a box across the floor of his cluttered office and pulled out one of his printed articles. "See what a fine job they do? I distribute them to my students and mail some to colleagues." He urged me to do the same. Of course I did not.

Barclay was a creature of habit. Every day he lunched at the Cornell faculty club. It was probably two hundred yards from his office in Sibley Hall, but he never walked there. He always drove. Days when I joined him for lunch, we would drive together. Finding a parking spot often took longer than walking there.

All of the planning students were graduate students, some Ph.D.s but mostly masters candidates. All were full-time students. The third floor of Sibley was devoted to shared offices for our students plus a geographical information system (GIS) lab. Sibley was open twenty-four hours a day, so there were always students around. On Friday afternoons, the department held a speaker series for students. A senior faculty member, the director of graduate studies, or DGS, was in charge, with assistance from one or two students, chauffeured speakers around and set up refreshments. Some speakers were professors from other universities, some were practicing urban planners, and some were officers of nonprofit organizations. All were radical. The students called that Friday speaker series "Cookies and Communism."

When Pierre Clavel became chair of our department, I took over as DGS. Thus I got to choose the speakers for the Friday speaker series. No more radicals. I selected empirical economists focused on urban issues. I was especially drawn to economists on the Federal Reserve staffs at the New York and the Chicago Feds. One reason was that the Fed did not allow their staff to accept honorariums as speakers, and it paid for their transportation costs. My speaker budget was meager. I also changed the refreshments from coffee, cookies and soft drinks to brie cheese, grapes, crackers, and cider.

One of my favorite faculty colleagues was José Lobo, a young brilliant assistant professor with a Ph.D. in urban planning from Cornell, but his true love was economics. While a graduate student, he took many courses from the economics department. He was far more enamored of neoclassical economics than I was at that time. I won him over to empirical analysis of urban issues. We collaborated on a number of refereed articles. He invited his favorite economics professor to make an informal presentation one evening to his Ph.D. students. I attended as well. I was appalled. The professor was a trailer-park Republican who trashed liberal opinions. The students nervously giggled at his non-PC remarks.

* * *

When we arrived in Ithaca, our daughter was almost two. We arranged for day care with a woman named Marie, who had about one-half dozen pre-school age kids of the law school faculty. Marie told us that she could have conversations with Erica, happily, but not with any other of her wards. The most common verbalization of the others was "Zach hits!" Zachary was a most unruly boy and continued so as he aged.

There was one bookstore in Ithaca, aside from the Cornell store, and it mirrored the tastes of my CRP faculty. One entire bookcase was devoted to feminist publications, another to gay literature. Only two shelves were dedicated to economics topics, and half of those were Marxist or radical. *New York Times* best sellers were not featured anywhere. Rumors of a Borders or Barnes and Noble store coming to Ithaca were welcomed by myself and others. The owner of Ithaca's sole bookstore wrote an op-ed in the *Ithaca Journal*, denouncing the nasty national bookstore chains because they would control what books were available for sale. I wrote a reply, pointing out that now one *person* decided what books to make available, the owner of the Ithaca bookstore.

A few years later, the editor of his quarterly book review publication chose to accept my positive review of *Money Makes the World Go Around* by Barbara Garson, famous for her hilarious spoof of President Johnson, *MacBird!* Soon after, that editor told me that the owner of the bookstore decided to reject my review. He had a long and vindictive memory.

When Erica was in first grade, she played soccer on a coed team of first graders in the autumn. The games were on Sunday afternoons, and we dutifully attended each game. Whenever her eager classmates of both teams rushed the ball, Erica held back. We quickly learned that soccer, or any contact sport, was not for her. She loved to swim. We spent each summer on a beautiful pond in Truro, Cape Cod. It was there that she learned to swim. While in elementary school we signed Erica up for a kids' swimming team. They practiced daily after school as well as in the summer. The coach, Roy Staley, was terrific. His team, elementary and high school kids, was highly rated in upstate New York. Erica made her very best friends on that swim team.

There were four departments of economics at Cornell. That may have reflected the fact that some colleges were parts of the State University of New York (SUNY) while the others were parts of the private Cornell University. The department of economics in the college of Literature Science and Arts was the only one so named and ignored the other three except when one or more of them became irksome, which was not infrequent. The one in the agriculture college was not surprisingly named Agriculture Economics. The one in industrial and labor relations was named Labor Economics. The one in the college of Human Ecology (formerly named Home Economics until the very idea of a branch of knowledge in such banal activities was widely ridiculed) was named Consumer Economics. The three colleges housing those three economics departments were all parts of the SUNY system.

In addition to those departments, there were many Ph.D. economists as faculty elsewhere at Cornell such as the business school, medical school, hotel school, and my small department, City and Regional Planning. Cornell is not *sui generis* in that regard. Economics has become an imperial scholarly field. Some of the most notable economists were not in the Department of Economics. For example, Robert Frank, well known as one of the leaders of behavioral economics, was in the Business School; Ron Ehrenberg, a leading light in labor economics was in the Industrial and Labor relations School; Walter Isard, the founder of the field of Regional Science was in my department, City and Regional Planning; Ravi Kanbur in Development Economics was in the College of Agriculture. The Department of Economics was specialized in economic theory. It never ranked in the top five economics departments of the nation. A continuing conflict while I was at Cornell was the determination of the Economics Department to gain some control over the economics programs elsewhere at the university. Central administration was, I believe, sympathetic to that goal. The other economics programs were much less so.

In my twelve years on the faculty at Cornell, I probably attended only two or three talks at the Department of Economics. One was to hear Edward Glaeser of Harvard, the star of urban economics. I do not remember his topic but I am certain it had an economic theory aspect. Another talk was from a rising star at the University of Minnesota, discussing his paper on the adverse impact of state labor laws upon firm location. Before he began his talk, he passed out a pamphlet on the advantages of "Right to Work" laws, which he enthusiastically supported. His paper examined the firm location effects along borders of states with no such anti-union laws and states with "Right to Work" laws. His results showed that many firms relocated from those with no such laws to those with them.

"Therefore, right to work law states promote economic efficiency," he asserted.

"Did you sort the movers and non-movers by industry?" I asked.

"No, I did not, it would make no difference."

I objected. "But firm location choices are affected by distance to their market, distance from suppliers, and weight-to-value ratios. For example, ready-mix cement firms must be near their market, breweries and newspaper printing plants with high-weight and low-value products must be close to their markets to minimize shipping costs, whereas firms with national and international customers and high-value products relative to weight could be indifferent to their location."

He brushed all that aside, asserting that, "For my purposes they could all be producing widgets."

I was the only audience member to raise such fundamental objections to his analysis of firm location choices without considering their industry. It was another example for me of oversimplification in neoclassical economic theory. One key reality absent from neoclassical economic theory is space or distance, as it was from classical economics.

One exciting talk I attended was sponsored by the Labor Economics Department in ILR. Two economic professors at distinguished departments, David Card and Alan B. Krueger, published a paper that challenged the timeless analysis from Econ 101 that minimum wage laws reduce employment of the low skilled. That conclusion is based upon a blackboard analysis, sans any empirical evidence. Card and Krueger had a natural experiment comparing employment at fast food restaurants on either side of a long state border, before and after one state raised its minimum wage. The data showed no *net* employment loss in the state that raised its minimum wage. As a shamelessly empirical economist suspicious of blackboard analyses, I was persuaded that they were right, given the caveat that the rise in the minimum wage was not substantial. As I arrived somewhat late for their packed presentation, I sat in the last row. A sheet was circulated asking for your name and affiliation. When the sheet came to me, the last person to sign, I noted that of the sixty or so faculty and students present, *none* were from the Department of Economics.

The Card and Krueger article caused an uproar, mostly negative, in the economics profession. Based on no evidence, I have an explanation of that uproar. Professors, especially those over fifty, are lazy when it comes to class preparation. If you have been teaching

Econ 101 for decades and suddenly one of your favorite blackboard exercises that pokes your thumb into the eyes of those mindless liberals is challenged, then you will be enraged. For support, let me quote Paul Krugman.

> "As an amateur anthropologist who has long studied that peculiar culture known as academic economics, it seems to me that an economic idea flourishes best if it is expressed in a rather technical way, even if the technical difficulty is largely spurious. After all, a teacher wants something to do at the blackboard, and a clever student wants something on which to demonstrate his or her cleverness." (Krugman, 1996, p. 16)

A year or so later, I read an interview with Card and Krueger in which they reported that they had lost friends because of their claims in that article. But not backing down, they published a book, *Myth and Measurement,* in 1995 in which they introduced more evidence that small increases in the minimum wage do not reduce employment. There is a national minimum wage of $7.50 per hour. Many states, and now cities, have their own minimum wage that is higher than the federal minimum.

In the autumn of 1994, Kathy was awarded a one-semester visiting scholar position at Princeton in the history department. Some of her scholarship on labor was historical. We rented a house in Princeton and enrolled Erica in first grade there. She was not happy about that move. To soothe her, to bribe her, we promised a puppy on our return to Ithaca in the spring if she would be a good sport about the move. She was. We had decided with her agreement that we would get her a Bernese Mountain dog, a handsome Swiss breed. Wisely, we borrowed one for a weekend from a kennel. Erica had an allergy reaction to the dog. I was glad about that because the dog was not playful. If you tossed a ball to it, the ball might as well have been invisible. I did not want a dumb dog. So we began a search for a dog she was not allergic to. We would take Erica to dog shelters, pick a likely candidate such as a poodle, and have her pet and play with the dog. No luck. She had allergic reactions. One breed reported to be the best hypoallergenic dog, the Portuguese Water Dog, looked like a shapeless pile of mud. No luck with that either. Then we moved away from purebred dogs.

At one shelter, we had Erica play with a beautiful half-breed, part German Shepherd and part Black Lab. Bingo. No allergic reaction after twenty-four hours. So we hurried back the next day and adopted that female dog. Erica already had a name for her. Happily reading the *American Girl* stories at the time, Erica chose Nellie, the name of an appealing orphan in the story, "Changes for Samantha". In fantasizing about getting a puppy, Erica assumed her dog would be cuddly. Nellie, although still a puppy, was too big for a seven-year-old to cuddle. But that was OK. We all loved Nellie.

* * *

The Labor Economics department held an event that was a weekend meeting of prominent labor economists from other universities. The location of the meeting rotated annually between Cornell and Princeton. I was invited to attend once by friends in Labor Economics. I remember a presentation by a labor economics star, whose name I cannot recall, from some other university. He was reviewing the history of academic labor economics, clearly celebrating the sunset of Institutional Economics and the rise of Neoclassical Economics. In the process he ridiculed the work of a prominent institutional economist at the Columbia business school, Eli Ginzberg. The ridicule won laughs from his audience, but not from me.

I had been a research scholar at Ginzberg's institute at Columbia, Conservation of Human Resources, for most of my years at NYU. My first grant that he won for me was from the U.S. Department of Labor to develop an econometric model of the New York City and region. Ginzberg himself was wary of econometric analysis, but he liked me. His institute was mainly funded by research grants from the Labor Department but also from private foundations such as the Rockefeller Brothers Fund and the Commonwealth Fund. Ginzberg was unabashedly liberal, an old New Dealer. I once heard him ridicule the Columbia economics department, decidedly neoclassical, as being out of touch with the real economic world. Perhaps he was nostalgic for the past when Columbia was dominated by the leading lights of Institutional Economics: Wesley Clair Mitchell, Arthur Burns, Karl Polanyi, and others. Mitchell founded the National Bureau of Economic Research (NBER) in 1920 and was the director of research there. He hired Columbia graduate students including Arthur Burns in 1930 and Milton Friedman in 1937. Simon Kuznets, the founder of national income accounts for the U.S., was at the NBER. The NBER was originally located in New York City, close to Columbia.

Ginzberg's institute withered in the 1990s. Grants from the U.S. Department of Labor had dried up, probably because young neoclassical economists at the Labor Department replaced aging institutional economists who liked Ginzberg's work. Ginzberg died in 2002. The NBER under new neoclassical economics leadership moved to Cambridge, close to Harvard and MIT.

Erica became a star swimmer under the tutelage of her coach, Roy. She was especially good at long-distance events and at the butterfly. We attended her events all over upstate New York. At one as she gained the lead in a butterfly race, one of her teammates rushed over to Roy sitting in a folding chair and not paying attention to the race, and shouted to him to watch Erica. He jumped up from his chair, knocking it over, and cheered Erica on. She won.

I paid keen attention when Erica was in an event. Otherwise I had my nose buried in a book. Swim meets are interminable, longer than baseball games. And swim meets in upstate New York are invariably indoors with uncomfortable bleacher seating. We always sat with parents of Erica's teammates. Given all the time *not* watching your own kid swim, some parents pursued other activities.

Two Cornell architecture professors with a daughter on the

team brought two boxes of applications for admission to one meet. We had become friends. Architecture and planning are in the same small Cornell college, Architecture, Art and Planning. Applicants for admission to architecture must submit portfolios of their art in addition to letters of recommendation and transcripts. As they pored over applications, I made a suggestion that would make their decisions easier. "Any kid who submits a painting or drawing of a sailboat, vase of flowers, or bowl of fruit should be rejected. So don't bother looking at the other material. Bold originality is what you want!"

For much of my stay at Cornell, Pierre Clavel was the Director of Graduate Studies or DGS, for the field of City and Regional Planning. That meant he oversaw admissions for masters and Ph.D. students, and distributed the financial aid to them. Cornell provided substantial financial aid to masters students because some of our competitors in planning, such as Berkeley and UCLA were state schools with much lower tuition. Pierre's process for distributing financial aid was egalitarian. Every American masters student got the same amount. Foreign students got zero. That was a university rule.

As DGS, Pierre also oversaw the curriculum. When I arrived at Cornell, I discovered that there was no required basic economics course for our masters students. To me, that was a shocking omission and I was determined to change that. I assembled the course requirements for urban planning masters students in other major planning programs around the nation. Not to my surprise, Cornell was the only one with *no* economics course requirement. A few had two required economics courses. At a faculty meeting I presented my evidence on what other planning programs did and proposed that we too should require a basic economics course. I had taught such a course at NYU for twenty years. The faculty was less than enthusiastic, although they begrudgingly agreed we were out of step with our competitors. I won.

On September 11, 2001, I was about to enter my classroom in Sibley Hall at Cornell when the department administrator told me that a passenger plane had crashed into one of the World Trade Center towers. I assumed it was an accident, and proceeded to teach my class. By the end of my class I learned that a second passenger plane crashed into the other tower. This was not an accident. We all saw on TV the collapse of the towers and before that the many helpless victims hurtling through windows to their certain death. About 3,000 people died from that terrorist attack, including hundreds of New York City firemen. I remember feeling numb, speechless, angry, and impotent rage. Over and over on TV that day were images of bodies hurtling out of the towers followed by their collapse.

As the initial shock faded after a few days, I stopped agonizing about the human victims and instead thought about the destroyed towers. They had been long in my life. We visited New York from Ithaca the next month, in late October. In Soho, north of the World Trade Center, the stench of smoke was ubiquitous. From all the places I would have seen the towers, I saw them no longer.

When the World Trade Center towers were completed in 1971, I was an assistant professor at NYU. I lived in an NYU high-rise apartment building on Bleecker Street. My tenth floor apartment faced south. At eye level, looking south in the foreground there was a forest of water tanks atop all the Soho buildings down to Canal Street. Beyond was the jumble of tall buildings, old and new, of Wall Street. And soaring above all of that were the twin towers of the World Trade Center. Bold, distinctive, dramatic, eminently noticeable, I saw them upon waking each morning, and I saw them lit up before falling asleep each night.

An overarching presence, like Mount Rainier must be to people in Seattle, but more sassy than grand because they were made in New York. There are no natural wonders in New York. All that is wondrous is unnatural.

My very young daughter Maureen also saw the World Trade Center from her bed each night and morning. When I would read to her a book she loved, *Goodnight Moon*, she would say at the end, "And goodnight twin towers."

When my daughter was in first grade at PS 41 in Greenwich Village, I would take her to the school bus stop each morning at the corner of Bleecker and La Guardia Place, from where the twin towers were in prominent view to the south. Frequently, a dispute would ensue. My daughter and the other children would insist that the North Tower, the nearer of the two, was taller than the South Tower. We parents would explain that they were the same height but one seemed taller because it was closer to us. My daughter and the other kids refused to accept that reasoning, trusting their senses more than their pedantic parents.

The first time I saw the towers up close, I was disappointed. I knew that they had been designed by Minoru Yamasaki. When I was growing up in Detroit, the motley collection of big houses and modest commercial buildings that formed Wayne State University was transformed by a set of Yamasaki buildings on the urban campus. I thought they were stunningly beautiful. The motif of narrow stone arches and tinted glass made them seem light, ethereal, almost of gossamer—the Alhambra in Detroit. The signature Yamasaki arches were repeated in the twin towers, but they topped out at maybe forty feet. Above was an endless sameness of vertical white stone. *A failure of imagination*, I thought; *too big to be beautiful.* Like Japanese gardeners who make exquisite little trees, what could they do with a redwood? Worse than the exterior was the plaza in front. A vast empty space—empty because it was uninviting. One would think the buildings were unoccupied. But underground, indoors, were warrens of shops, mobs of people, and the frenetic pace of New York.

I had occasion to go to the towers a few times a year while I lived in New York and taught at NYU. I was an economic consultant for the Port Authority, and I sometimes went to the New York State Labor Department located in the towers to get employment data. The offices I visited were bright open spaces, and the windows were always clean. (There is nothing so dreary as a New York office with dirty windows.)

Not only were they clean, but they were prominently visible from everywhere except the center corridors where the elevators were located. In the Port Authority and Labor Department offices, only the corner offices were walled off from the rest of the space, so one could see the windows everywhere. That struck me as wonderfully egalitarian. Riding the twin tower elevators was as much fun as amusement park thrill rides.

In 1974 a remarkable and zany event brought them local and national attention for a moment. A French high-wire artist, Philippe Petit, managed, *sans* any official approval, to run a thin steel cable between the tops of the towers and walked across holding a balancing pole—with no net, of course. His bold exploit was shown on the evening news everywhere. I loved it. I think all New Yorkers loved it.

The year 1976 was the 200th anniversary of the nation's founding. Part of the celebration was the assembly in New York harbor of the tall ships—twenty or so three- and four-masted sailing ships from around the world. That majestic spectacle was the featured event on national television on July 4th, 1976, and the twin towers appeared prominently. They became the signature of New York.

In the 1980s the restaurant at the top of one of the towers, Windows on the World, very rarely had empty tables. Al Shanker, the president of the United Federation of Teachers back then, told me that Clay Falker offered to take him to lunch there one afternoon. Falker was the editor of *New York Magazine*, and he had his secretary call to make a reservation for that day, not failing to mention the names of the host and guest. The *maitre de* apologized and said that Mr. Falker and his guest could be accommodated in one month, not sooner.

I went there for a Sunday brunch with some of my wife's family on a sunny winter day in 1984. The sensation of looking *down* on the Brooklyn Bridge and other landmarks of lower Manhattan made me giddy. How could one be blasé in such a spectacular aerie? I remember that the food was good, the piano playing sophisticated, and the champagne cold and crisp. But they were minor accoutrements to the main event: the view.

On returning to New York by car after a visit to family in the Midwest, the twin towers would come into view from the highway in New Jersey long before any other Manhattan site, announcing that a weary journey was nearly over. I was always happy to see them. My home, my bed, was only a few miles from that landmark. Years later, when I lived in Brooklyn, I sometimes would bike to NYU on glorious spring or autumn days. Riding across the Brooklyn Bridge, I could see both the twin towers and the Statue of Liberty awash in sunlight.

In the winter of 1993, I had occasion to drive from Ithaca to a Bloomingdale's warehouse in a rented truck to pick up two sofas we had purchased. The warehouse was located off the spur of the New Jersey Turnpike leading to the Holland Tunnel, a few miles from Manhattan. While rumbling along in the empty truck almost at my destination, I suddenly heard sirens. Behind me was a string of emergency vehicles—ambulances and fire trucks—hell-bent for the Holland Tunnel with sirens screaming and red lights flashing. I pulled over, letting them whiz by. I counted twenty-one emergency vehicles. Something terrible had happened, but I did not know what. It was February 23rd, 1993, the day a bomb blast was set off by Arab terrorists in the World Trade Center garage.

In July of 2001, Larry Silverstein signed a long-term lease for the World Trade Center with the Port Authority, taking over as landlord for ninety-nine years. He paid $3.2 billion for that lease. He apparently anticipated high rents and full offices far into the future.

Sleep, always easy for me, became fitful after the World Trade Center was destroyed on September 11, 2001. All of those sudden horrible deaths numb the imagination. A few moments after waking each morning, I would remember that it happened and become depressed. I did not lose any friends; people I knew who worked there got out or were not inside when it happened. But I have lost something that was long in my life. Not something as impersonal as a monument, but rather a big visible piece of the loud, rude, vibrancy that is New York.

We had planned our October trip to New York City before 9/11. Strolling around Soho after brunch with friends, the smell of smoke was strong. We then went uptown. That Saturday afternoon at the Metropolitan Museum, many people lounged on the steps in the autumn sun. Inside there were crowds at the Signac exhibition, in the shop, and in the coat check line. Finding an empty taxi was as challenging as ever. The theater district restaurant was full and bustling. All the seats for *Phantom of the Opera* were filled. I had bought tickets weeks in advance but even so, I could not get orchestra seats. After the theater, in an Upper West Side market crowded with shoppers near midnight, an Arab woman cashier in a hijab was cheerfully dealing with grumpy impatient customers.

The following weekend, the New York Marathon proceeded as scheduled ages in advance, with 30,000 runners packed together on the Verrazzano Bridge. The mayor dared not cancel the event despite concerns for security. Nothing happened. Peaceful sleep returned after that trip. I realized—I saw—that they took out a piece, but only a piece, of New York.

Davydd Greenwood, a sociology professor at Cornell, and his Norwegian collaborator had a grant to analyze the shortcomings of modern social science. They planned a book covering most social sciences. The first chore was to round up experts in each field to contribute a chapter. Davydd was turned down by the Cornell economics professor he selected, perhaps more than one, and so he turned to me. Why me, I do not know. I was not a famous economics professor. Perhaps the famous professor or professors he wanted were too busy or perhaps they were loath to express any shortcomings of economics. By then, the early 2000s, I was eager to write about the shortcomings of neoclassical economics.

I wrote an article for that project that I entitled "Economics: Diminishing Marginal Utility." It was published in the journal *Challenge* in 2006, which is well known for articles critical of neoclassical economics. In the first few pages, I praised the effects of economists upon some public policy issues such as introducing

Section 8 vouchers for public housing, a program that helped to reduce racial discrimination with rent subsidies for the poor rather than constructing new public housing.

What I beat up on was the disastrous consequences of American economists advising Russia on transitioning to a capitalist economy. It did not work because they stressed privatization of industries before establishing the strict rule of law common to all rich capitalist nations.

Capitalism does not work without laws and without institutions to enforce laws. But the economists cavalierly assumed that the rule of law could come later. They trusted the market and competition to sort out ownership of newly privatized firms. But the corrupt government sold existing industries at fire sale prices to the former soviet managers. The absence of "government interference" (among the strong assumptions of neoclassical economics listed in the early part of this book) led to the overnight formation of monopolies. It is a tragedy for Russia that its government turned to American economists to transform its state-owned economy to a capitalist economy. Instead its government should have turned to Chinese economists for designing a transition to capitalism, because China has successfully done that. Part of the secret of their success is that the transition has been gradual, whereas in Russia it was imposed overnight.

Andrei Shleifer, a Harvard economist who won the prestigious John Bates Clark Medal, was the chief architect of the transition plan for Russia. He ran into legal problems for his work there.

> ". . . the U.S. Justice Department in 2000 brought suit against Harvard University, Shleifer, and three others relating to their work for Russia funded by federal grants. In 2004 the judge found that 'Harvard economics professor Shleifer and attorney Hay had conspired to defraud the U.S. government, engaged in self-dealing and violated conflict of interest regulations' . . . Harvard agreed to pay . . . $26.5 million. Shleifer agreed to pay $2 million . . . Less than a year after that settlement, Lawrence Summers, friend and defender of Shleifer, announced that he was stepping down as president of Harvard." ("Economics: Diminishing Marginal Utility," *Challenge,* Sept.-Oct. 2006, p. 85)

Harvard University appointed a faculty committee to determine if Shleifer should be penalized. The outcome was not publicized so we do not know. We do know that Shleifer was not fired.

I also beat up on a hare-brained scheme in the Defense Department to launch a futures market for terrorist acts. Two senators exposed the plan to the public.

> "The resulting uproar led Defense to abandon the plan, as well as force out the convicted felon Admiral John Poindexter (the retired Navy admiral who was fired as Reagan's national security advisor and was convicted of conspiracy, lying to Congress, defrauding the government, and destroying

> evidence in the Iran-contra affair) who oversaw that plan . . . Not to my surprise, I learned that the plan was the brainchild of an assistant professor of economics . . . at George Mason University, the place where public choice theory was born." ("Economics: Diminishing Marginal Utility," *Challenge*, Sept.-Oct. 2006, pp. 85–86)

The lesson here recalls the maxim of the late liberal economist Arthur Okun: "The market needs a place, and the market needs to be kept in its place."

Winters are long in Ithaca. It is not as cold as Wisconsin and Minnesota, but it is not as sunny. Many people who live in Ithaca suffer from the affliction brought on by absence of sunlight. Because the winters are so long there, I took up downhill skiing when I was over fifty. I needed something recreational to do. Biking was good in the spring, when it finally arrived, but not in the winter. Most days of classes I walked to work, about one mile from my home. As I aged, I noted a change in that habit in the winter. Rather than entering the long Sibley Hall at the far door near my office, I entered at the near door at the end of my walk to get out of the cold.

A young aggressive urban planning professor, Rolf Pendall, was hired by my Cornell department, City and Regional Planning, around 1995. He won a grant from the Brookings Institute to write an analysis of upstate New York and he hired me to do the part on the upstate economy. As I did the necessary research, I realized that there was no good news. Population had been declining for a few decades. Buffalo, the second biggest city after New York, had been a major center of the steel industry, and that industry had been in national decline for many years. Rochester, the headquarters of Kodak, Xerox, and Bausch & Lomb was in trouble from foreign competition. Kodak never recovered from the double whammy of Fuji Film and the shift to digital photography. Xerox, whose name became a verb in American English, was losing sales to both foreign and domestic competitors. The headquarters was moved from Rochester to Connecticut.

Remember when IBM, another upstate New York firm, built mainframe computers? Much of that production was done in upstate New York around Elmira. Although IBM did build personal computers, they lost that market to Dell and to Apple. Carrier Air Conditioning has moved most of its production from Syracuse, New York to China. Even the dairy farms in upstate New York have been hit. They were part of a compact of northeastern states which put a floor under milk prices. Congress limited the duration of its authorization in 1999, and the compact ended in 2001.

So, the report I wrote was a grim story of economic decline in upstate New York. The final report that Brookings published was an optimistic story of economic resurgence. In reading it, I kept thinking of the Monty Python film, *The Life of Brian* which ends with dozens of crucified men singing "Always Look at the Bright Side of Life." Years later I learned from a former Brookings economist that the once-independent Brookings Institute ran out of money from its founders and was now supported by outside grants. Perhaps the governor of New York paid for our study, and Brookings edited it to please the sponsor.

Chapter Twenty-Four

UCLA

The weather was one factor that made me weary of Ithaca and Cornell. For much of our married life we had lived in New York City, and Kathy and I started to miss a big city. Our daughter Erica was very happy in Ithaca because of her friends and swim team. When she was a high school freshman in Ithaca, 2003 to 2004, the UCLA Law School began aggressively recruiting Kathy. She was tempted to accept their offer. Erica was dead set against leaving Ithaca.

At sixty-seven years old, I did not want to start looking for a new academic job. In our years at Cornell we had gone off for visiting professor positions for Kathy at Stanford and at Yale, either of which she preferred to Cornell. But she did not get an offer from those schools. Being fifty-five years old, she realistically viewed the UCLA offer as her last chance to leave Cornell for a better academic position. I agreed. Law schools usually recruit senior faculty with a one-year visit and then decide whether to make a permanent offer. Kathy told the UCLA Law School that she would not accept a visiting professor position. That in part reflected Erica's reasonable objection to leaving her friends and her team for one year and then returning. She had lost friends on our Stanford and Yale visits. "Either we go for good or we do not go!" Erica cried.

In January 2004, the three of us flew to Los Angeles at UCLA's expense to look at houses, schools, and to meet faculty. That morning the temperature in Ithaca had soared up to eight degrees Fahrenheit. When we arrived in Los Angeles, the rental car attendant said, "We do not have the sedan you requested. Would you consider taking a convertible?" So for the next few days we drove around L.A. with the top down, visiting private schools for Erica, looking at houses, and meeting faculty. Erica's head was turned by one of the four schools we interviewed, Harvard-Westlake. That was great for us because we secretly preferred it over the other schools. It was a no-nonsense academic institution with a fine record of admissions to Ivy League colleges. The school was to be Erica's choice, not ours, and being a serious student, she chose it.

Finding a house was not so easy. We had agreed that if we had to get on a freeway to get to UCLA each day, we would stay at Cornell. We saw some good houses in the Hancock Park neighborhood of L.A. within reach of UCLA without using a freeway. But the trip might take forty-five minutes on weekdays. So we bit the bullet and started looking in the Westwood neighborhood where UCLA was located. House prices were much higher there. We ended up buying a beautiful Spanish colonial house in Westwood that was on a dead-end street, one-and-a-half miles from UCLA.

A position for me was the last issue. The Law School arranged for me to give a talk to the UCLA urban planning faculty. That was a success that led to the offer of a three-year visiting professor position, not a tenured permanent position. Why would any department offer a tenured position to someone sixty-seven years old? The NYU economics department would if the person was a famous scholar, but I was not. I would be seventy at the end of my visiting professor position. I did not love the idea of retiring, but something else might develop for me. So Kathy and I accepted the UCLA offers.

In September 2004, we left Ithaca for Los Angeles. In Erica's first week at Harvard-Westlake she reported to us, crestfallen, "You know, I think I might be the dumbest kid in that school." She turned out to be one of the smartest kids in that school, and captain of their swim team in her senior year. About swimming, I thought that since all the U.S. Olympic swimmers I ever heard of were from California or Florida, Erica would be out of her league in California. It was not true.

Another thing not true: my expectation about UCLA students. Given that Cornell was an Ivy League school and UCLA was a state school, I thought both the graduate students and the undergraduates at UCLA would be inferior to Cornell students. They were not, I was happy to realize.

There was a cultural difference that disturbed me at first. At NYU and Cornell and Chicago, students always addressed me as Professor Drennan. At UCLA I was Matt. I got used to it.

Before UCLA, I had never been at a university that had a

department of geography. The geography department at UCLA was ranked number one in the U.S. Some of their faculty were economic geographers who became good friends, Alan Scott and David Rigby. Another geographer in the urban planning department, Michael Storper, also became a good friend. I dropped my subscription to the *Journal of Regional Science* once I realized that I was more interested in what economic geographers were writing about and subscribed to the *Journal of Economic Geography.*

Before discovering economic geography at UCLA, I became interested in agglomeration economies addressed by many urban economists. An agglomeration economy is an unmeasured advantage that accrues to firms in the same or related industries located in the same labor market, city or metropolitan area. The most famous British economist of the nineteenth century, Alfred Marshall, was the first to write about agglomeration economies. The topic was ignored for some decades until urban economists and regional science scholars resurrected it in the current era.

But unfortunately, economists, and less so regional science scholars, are obsessed with manufacturing. So most economics articles about agglomeration economies focus upon manufacturing and sometimes retail trade. To paraphrase the popular song, they are "Looking for agglomeration economies in all the wrong places."

As already noted, most of my published work focuses upon producer services or information intensive industries in cities and metropolitan areas. One characteristic of such firms is a tendency to cluster in space: finance and publishing in New York, computer software in Silicon Valley, entertainment in Los Angeles. The fact that they tend to cluster strongly suggests that they gain something from proximity, namely agglomeration economies. I discovered at UCLA that economic geographers have *not* overlooked agglomeration economies in producer service firms. They recognize that tacit knowledge shared over drinks after work among people in the same business is valuable and keeps clusters viable.

The dean of my small college at UCLA, Social Welfare, Planning, and Public Policy (now named the Luskin School), was awarded a grant by the Los Angeles Chamber of Commerce and The Urban League to produce a report on economic development in Los Angeles. The dean designated his assistant dean, Bill Plant, the director of that research. Bill chose me and one of our best Ph.D. students, Taner Osman, to be on that grant.

Because of my awful experience with the Brookings grant at Cornell, I insisted that the sponsors could *not* edit our final report. Bill agreed emphatically, and that was written into the contract. The agreed plan was for us to present our findings in three public meetings the sponsors would arrange. My domain would be economic development issues in Los Angeles, including taxes. Taner's domain would be the problem of firms departing Los Angeles for other places including other states.

I greatly enjoyed doing the research on economic development. I did not limit it to what economic development efforts had been adopted in Los Angeles. I studied what worked and what failed in other states and cities over the past few decades—some version of so-called "enterprise zones." An enterprise zone was a low-income neighborhood, usually a minority neighborhood, with very few private sector firms and high unemployment. The goal was to shower firms that relocated to a designated enterprise zone with government subsidies and additional subsidies for hiring local unemployed residents, thus lifting up the neighborhood's economy.

But the goal was never achieved. Some firms moved in to get the relocation subsidy, and then moved out. Those that stayed very often could not find local residents with the skills required for the offered jobs. Postmortem studies of enterprise zones showed that the government's expenditure per job created in an enterprise zone was extremely high. No bang for their buck.

One of the two sponsors of our study, the Urban League, was determined that we should promote enterprise zones in minority neighborhoods of Los Angeles. But my research concluded that that was a bad idea. The other sponsor, the Chamber of Commerce, was alarmed by reports of firms moving out of Los Angeles. Their proposed solution to stopping the move-outs was to reduce business taxes. Taner's careful research with an awesome data base on firm relocation over many years showed that employment at firms moving *into* Los Angeles was about the same as employment at firms moving out of Los Angeles.

I presented my research results at the first public meeting the sponsors had arranged, and I believe Taner presented his results on relocation at the second public meeting. After that doubly bad news for the sponsors, they cancelled the third public meeting. Did they complain to the dean? I have no idea. But we spoke truth to power; the best that academics can do.

Rising Income Inequality

Paul Krugman, *The New York Times* columnist and winner of the Nobel Memorial award in economics, is my favorite economist. In 2007 he published a book, *The Conscience of a Liberal,* in which he documented the drastic rise of income inequality in the United States over the past few decades. His explanation of that trend was vague: institutional changes. I wanted to know why it happened. Then I discovered the article, "Winner-Take-All Politics" (later a book), by Jacob S. Hacker and Paul Pierson, both political scientists. The scales fell from my eyes. They convinced me that the rise of inequality was due to political factors, not economic factors. Among them was the huge increase in Washington lobbying by corporations beginning in the 1970s, the rise of well-funded right wing think tanks, and the failure to enforce labor laws. My own past work on the ending of income convergence in metropolitan areas persuaded me that part of that story was raising national income inequality. Both trends began in the late 1970s and early 1980s.

At UCLA I began to work on a book manuscript on income inequality. Yale University Press published it in 2015, *Income Inequality: Why It Matters and Why Most Economists*

Did Not Notice. Most economists did not notice because they were wedded to Milton Friedman's flawed theory of consumption, which quickly replaced Keynes theory of consumption.

One of the central ideas in Keynes great book, *The General Theory of Employment, Interest and Money,* is the average propensity to consume (APC), that is, the percent of personal income that consumers spend. Lacking data on personal income and consumption when his book was published in 1936, he reasoned that the long-term upward trend of consumer spending would not match the long-term upward trend of consumers' personal income. Thus the APC would decline over time. Milton Friedman challenged Keynes's view in his book, *A Theory of the Consumption Function* (1957). The data he had available at the time (excluding the 1920s) supported his argument that the APC was stable over time. And if APC was stable over time, he reasoned, there was no basis for thinking that the distribution of income played any role in aggregate consumption expenditures, the largest component of gross domestic product (GDP).

Friedman won the day. His theory of consumption was adopted in neoclassical economics, and the distribution of income became irrelevant. But then something strange happened. Beginning in the mid 1980s, thirty years after Friedman's book was published, the APC *rose* for two decades (ignoring recessions), hitting a peak in 2005 before the Great Recession. Why did that happen? Because consumers took on enormous debt to maintain their consumption in the face of stagnant or declining incomes. As I argued in my book:

> ". . . the mainstream theory of consumption, which posits no role for income inequality in the economy, is seriously flawed. The story here is that increasing consumer indebtedness, which supported consumption until the crash in 2008–09, was driven by the pressure of most households to maintain consumption in the face of stagnant income as income inequality relentlessly rose for thirty years or so. That debt-supported expansion of consumption became unsustainable after 2007 once house prices tumbled." (p. 3)
>
> Here is how I conclude that book:
>
> "Finally, I present a plea for a more fact-based economics than an authority-based economics. In the 1960s when it became clear that the APC, and of course the saving rate [1-APC] were stable despite rapid income growth, Keynes's concern that income growth would lower the APC . . . was jettisoned by macroeconomists. That was the right choice, and it was based on evidence. Starting in the mid-1980s, the APC began its long rise . . . which continued for 20 years." (pp. 131-132).

In the 2013 edition of his popular economics text, Gregory

Mankiw argues that the APC will be stable over long time periods: "Hence in long time-series, one should observe a constant average propensity to consume, as in fact Kuznets found." (Mankiw, 2013, *Macroeconomics,* 8th edition, Houndmills, p. 483)

"Did he look at the data? Why have today's economists failed to jettison the mainstream theory of consumption in the face of so much evidence to the contrary?" (p. 132)

Conclusion

As I noted earlier in this memoir, I had hoped my first academic job after earning my Ph.D. would be in an economics department. But I settled for a tenure track position at NYU in the graduate school of public administration, now the Wagner School. My entire academic career has been in public policy departments (NYU) or urban planning (Cornell and UCLA). In retrospect, I am glad that I never served in an economics department, for reasons I hope I have made clear. I fear that I would have remained an earnest believer in neoclassical economics as I was upon earning my Ph.D.

Looking back, I am relieved that I jettisoned all that.

Made in United States
Troutdale, OR
11/03/2026

56844520R00120